OPTIMUM PERFORMANCE TRAINING:

BASKETBALL

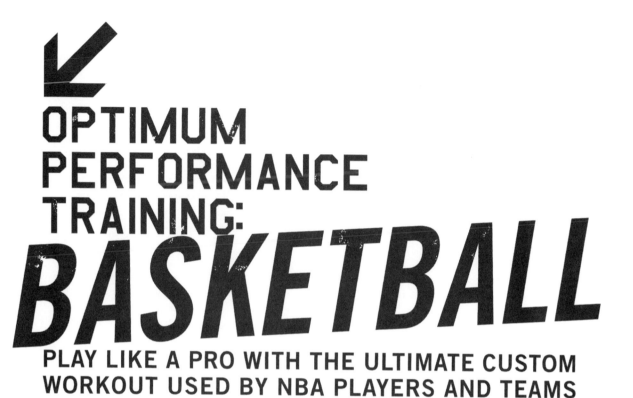

OPTIMUM PERFORMANCE TRAINING: BASKETBALL

PLAY LIKE A PRO WITH THE ULTIMATE CUSTOM WORKOUT USED BY NBA PLAYERS AND TEAMS

MICHEAL CLARK DPT, MS, PT

with Caroline San Juan, MSM

ReganBooks
An Imprint of HarperCollins*Publishers*

The information in this book has been carefully researched, and all efforts have been made to ensure accuracy. The author and the publisher assume no responsibility for any injuries suffered or damages or losses incurred during or as a result of following the exercise program in this book. All of the exercises and procedures should be carefully studied and clearly understood before attempting them at home. Always consult your physician or qualified medical professional before beginning this or any exercise program.

HarperCollins books may be purchased for educational, business, or sales promotional use. For information please write: Special Markets Department, HarperCollins Publishers Inc., 10 East 53rd Street, New York, NY 10022.

FIRST EDITION

Designed by Richard Ljoenes
Illustrations by Scott Dalrymple
Equipment photographs courtesy of Perform Better

Printed on acid-free paper

Library of Congress Cataloging-in-Publication Data

Clark, Micheal.
    Optimum performance training : basketball : play like a pro with the ultimate custom workout used by NBA players and teams / Micheal Clark with Caroline San Juan.—1st ed.
        p. cm.
    ISBN 13: 978-0-06-085223-8
    ISBN 10: 0-06-085223-2
    1. Basketball—Training. I. San Juan, Caroline. II. Title.

GV885.35.C53 2006
613.7'11—dc22

                                                              2005055182

06 07 08 09 10 WBC/RRD 10 9 8 7 6 5 4 3 2 1

This book is dedicated to our families and friends,
and the colleagues and athletes who helped
develop the OPT System.

CONTENTS

FOREWORD

I have one thing to say about Dr. Mike Clark; he is the Michael Jordan of sports medicine and I have no doubt that he will change the face of conditioning throughout the entire sports world with his Optimum Performance Training (OPT) System.

I met with Dr. Clark in Phoenix several years ago. I wanted to improve my game—to become injury-free and move better on the court. Dr. Clark instructed me to take several walking steps away from him; then he told me to turn and walk back toward him. It was unbelievable; from that short stroll, Dr. Clark was able to tell me which muscles were weak, which were tight, and what I needed to do to fix them. I was ready to hop on a plane and follow him to the National Academy of Sports Medicine in California so I could train with him. Fortunately, I didn't have to—Dr. Clark brought his OPT System to the Phoenix Suns when he became the team's sports-medicine and sports-performance consultant. I have trained with his system ever since.

Amazingly, I have not missed a game in 4 years, and I credit this to Dr. Clark and OPT. Let me tell you why. You know the saying that you're only as strong as your weakest link? Well, it's true. What makes the OPT System so effective is that it uses a structured system to identify your body's weaknesses. That's the starting point. From there the program strengthens these weaknesses and conditions your entire body for optimum performance.

The traditional programs I trained with in the past left me stiff and tight. I never felt stretched the way I needed to be. They also didn't focus on conditioning my core—I'm not even sure I knew what it was. The core is the foundation of your body, and also the foundation of the OPT System. Once I started training it, every other part of my body became easier to work with.

The OPT System is difficult and easy at the same time. It's difficult at first because you do stretches and exercises that you've never done before—it's different from any other style of training. But then you get the hang of it, and it becomes easier and more interesting and challenging. What I like most is that everyone's body is treated individually with this program. The exercises are tailored for me—they make me stronger and able to work harder so I can build my body to be as efficient as it can be.

The OPT System would be beneficial to the recreational player and the high school and college athlete. Kids will respond even more quickly than the professional who didn't have the benefit of the OPT System before reaching the NBA. Using this system, young athletes can lay the groundwork for a healthy body that will hold up throughout all their basketball years. This way they can avoid the pain and problems of a person who has played in the NBA for years.

An NBA season is seven months and can be longer. I am on the court for more than 40 minutes a night. I thank Dr. Clark for knowing how the body works and creating a system that trains me effectively. Now I can play my best throughout the whole year—injury free. Someday soon, people all over the world will be training with the OPT System—and I think that's very exciting!

STEPHON MARBURY

New York Knicks

Two-Time NBA All-Star

INTRODUCTION

I'm sure you've heard the phrase, *the results speak for themselves*. I couldn't agree more with that statement, which is why I'll let the results of star guard Stephon Marbury speak for the effectiveness of the Optimum Performance Training (OPT) System:

- Stephon has increased his vertical jump by 5 inches!
- He has not been injured or missed a game in the last four years.

I'm frequently asked why I created the OPT System. The answer is simple: after seeing one athlete after another come to me with the same set of problems, I decided to do something to prevent these common injuries from happening in the first place.

You see, most athletes have the misconception that if they make their muscles bigger, they will play better and prevent injury. But this is not necessarily true. I'll explain.

My doctoral studies in human movement science confirmed that athletes who get injured or perform poorly have three weaknesses in common:

1. MUSCLE IMBALANCE: when muscles on one side of a joint tighten, muscles on the opposite side weaken, causing pain and poor function of the joint.

2. POOR CORE STABILITY: weakness throughout the supportive muscles of the pelvis, hip, and spine—the foundation muscles of your body.

3. POOR BALANCE: the inability to recruit the right muscles at the right time.

Strength training and developing bigger muscles does not correct the weaknesses listed above. That's not to suggest that you should skip strength conditioning. It has its place in an overall conditioning program. But it should not be the *only* component in your program.

The athletic trainers of the National Basketball Athletic Trainers Association (NBATA) have adopted the OPT System as their model for performance enhancement and injury prevention. This system of training is also being used by players such as NBA MVPs Steve Nash, Shaquille O'Neal, and Kevin Garnett, NBA All-Stars Stephon Marbury and Shawn Marion, and Rookies of the Year Emeka Okafor and Amare Stoudemire. Teams such as the Phoenix Suns, which led the NBA in the fewest games missed due to injury and premiered their starters in an astonishing 97 percent of regular season games during the 2004–2005 season, are also training with this system. This book will unveil to you the OPT System used by these star athletes and teams and will teach you how to:

1. Identify, correct, and prevent muscle imbalances, poor core strength, and poor balance.

2. Focus on conditioning your *stability* muscles in addition to your strength and power muscles.

3. Train your heart and lungs specifically for basketball.

By following this system, step-by-step, as outlined in this book, you will soon be enjoying these improvements on the court.

Five more inches on your vertical could be the difference between coming down hard with a rebound or just coming down hard. You choose!

Play hard, play smart, and have fun!

DR. MICHEAL A. CLARK, DPT, MS, PT, NASM-PES

CEO/President of the National Academy of Sports Medicine (NASM)

Part I
THE SETUP

ONE

What Is Optimum Performance Training (OPT)?

If you want to be a great basketball player, you have to train your body the way it moves on the court. You're probably thinking cardio, strength, and power training, to be stronger, faster, more explosive, and agile. All true. But there is one component of basketball fitness that has often been overlooked: Stability Training.

What is so important about Stability Training? Imagine a car that can go 150 mph; but the brakes only stop up to 50 mph. How fast would you drive the car? Probably not even 50 mph. On the court, your body is like the car. If you have strong muscles and the ability to move fast but you don't have good brakes, you will always perform less than your best. The stabilizing muscles are your brakes.

The OPT System has yielded phenomenal results with top NBA athletes because it trains both the brakes and high performance capabilities of the athlete. Some players have increased their speed by over 30 percent, while ankle, knee, and back injuries have dropped by more than 55 percent! Just this past season the Phoenix Suns had only forty-one games missed due to injury while the NBA average was over one hundred games missed! The Suns credit a large part of this success to their players' improved ability to stabilize, decelerate, and accelerate in all directions as a result of the OPT system.

This book will unveil the training system used by many NBA teams, players, and sports medicine professionals so that you can enjoy the same phenomenal improvements in your game. You will do exercises that you have never seen or even imagined before, but don't let that intimidate you. This book will guide you step-by-step through these exercises with a complete, easy to use training system that will condition you for your personal *best* on the court.

First, you need to understand a few basic principles about your body. Your body has three different types of muscles:

1. STABILITY MUSCLES: the small, deep muscles that support your joints and muscles so you can balance and perform strength and power movements on the court. The deep muscles that connect and support the pelvis and spine are examples of stability muscles.

2. STRENGTH MUSCLES: the large, superficial muscles like the chest, back, shoulder, and butt muscles that enable you to be as strong as possible in defense and rebound positions.

3. POWER MUSCLES: the muscles you recruit at the right time to execute the exact amount of force and speed needed to perform explosive moves like a lay-up or dunk. These movements are made using a combination of stability and strength muscles.

As you see in the illustration below, stability muscles are the foundation of the OPT program because they are the foundation of your muscular system. Without strong stability muscles, you cannot have optimum strength or power. That's because your body uses stability muscles in conjunction with strength muscles to execute strength movements. Similarly, your body uses a combination of stability, strength, and power muscles to perform a power movement. OPT progressively conditions for stability, strength, and power in three phases of training:

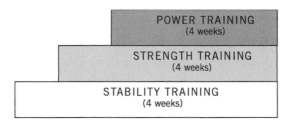

The OPT System

STABILITY TRAINING: HOW TO SHUT DOWN THE POST-UP, AND THINK *INSIDE* THE BOX

As the foundation of OPT, Stability Training conditions some of the most fundamental muscles of your body—your stability muscles. These muscles are key to preventing injuries and maximizing strength and power moves on the court. If Amare Stoudemire didn't train his stability muscles, you'd never see him boxing out guys in the paint, because he just wouldn't have the capability to move laterally the way he does.

In basketball, your ankle, knee, and back joints take the brunt of forceful movements like jumping and landing. Your stability muscles support these joints and protect them from injury. They also provide the foundation from which your strength and power muscles produce force.

The deep supporting muscles give you endurance to hold your body in a particular position for an extended period of time. On the court, they allow you to maintain a squatlike position while you are playing defense by engaging the muscles of your hips and spine. When Amare Stoudemire trolls around under the basket, he's constantly hunkered down, ready to move in any direction. If your stability muscles are weak, you will fatigue quickly and lose your defensive edge.

Surprisingly, most basketball conditioning programs mistakenly skip Stability Training and jump straight into Strength Training. This frequently leads to injury because the joints and stability muscles have not been conditioned for strength movements. The OPT System, however, attributes its success in great part to dedicating as much time and effort to Stability Training as it does to Strength and Power Training. In fact, adding Stability Training into his workouts is one of the key reasons Stephon Marbury has not missed a game in 4 years!

So you will begin your OPT program in this phase by using light weight, high repetitions, and unstable exercises like the Single-Leg Squat (illustrated below) to stimulate and condition the stability muscles.

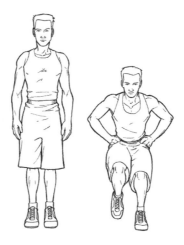

There's a bonus to training in this phase, by the way. You burn more calories than in Strength and Power Training because you recruit a lot of muscles with this type of conditioning. That means you will also get leaner by knocking off excess body fat, making you appear more muscular.

Your Stability Training program will be detailed in Chapter 7. After four weeks of training in this phase, you will progress to Strength Training.

STRENGTH TRAINING: HOW TO STAY IN THE PAINT AND DEFEND AGAINST THE PICK LIKE SHAQ

The second phase of training is Strength Training. The goal of this phase is to make your major muscles like the chest, back, shoulders, and thighs stronger and bigger.

On the court, strength is important with movements like posting someone up. Imagine Emeka Okafor's elbow digging into your back, trying to keep you out of the paint. You need to have strong lower body and trunk muscles to maintain your position against a strong opponent.

Strength Training uses heavier weight and lower repetitions than Stability Training. Your Strength Training program will be detailed in Chapter 8. After four weeks in this phase, you will progress to Power Training.

POWER TRAINING: HOW TO BANG THE BOARDS, SLAM DUNK, AND BURY THE JUMPER

This phase is the *optimum* in the Optimum Performance Training System, because it uses both stability and strength muscles to execute quick, explosive power moves like a lay-up or dunk. Michael Jordan is the classic example of a player who reached *optimum* conditioning. Stability, strength, and power worked together seamlessly as he maneuvered down the court to elude defenders and create an incomparable acrobatic shot—be it a fade-away jumper, a spectacular slam dunk, or a spinning lay-up. His stability, strength, and power also made him a threat as one of the best one-on-one defenders in the game.

This is what Power Training is all about. You will use the stability and strength gains you made and combine them with power. The result will undoubtedly be your *optimum* performance on the court.

You will condition for power in this phase by lifting heavy weight in a controlled manner, immediately followed by a fast basketball-type movement with little or no weight. This is exactly the type of workout NBA athletic trainers are doing with players such as Amare Stoudemire and Emeka Okafor. They will perform a strength exercise like a Squat, immediately followed by a power move like a Squat Jump (illustrated on pages 173 and 175). The results? Amare Stoudemire and Emeka Okafor have both enjoyed the honor of being awarded NBA Rookie of the Year.

Your Power Training program will be detailed in Chapter 9. After four weeks in this phase, you will return to the beginning of the OPT system and repeat all three phases again. Hey, nobody said it would be easy.

KEY POINT

You have three types of muscles:

1. *STABILITY* MUSCLES

2. *STRENGTH* MUSCLES

3. *POWER* MUSCLES

These muscles have to be trained specifically, *progressively*, and continuously.

TWO

How to Use This Book

Imagine increasing your range of motion by 50 percent, or increasing your total body strength more than 25 percent! The key to these amazing results is the *correct* use of the OPT System. NBA players like Steve Nash have significantly improved stability, strength, and power by *correctly* following this program. This chapter will explain how to use this book to guide you through your OPT program.

By now you know that your body has three different types of muscles. Each of these muscles is conditioned in the OPT System's three phases of training.

STABILITY TRAINING: Trains stability muscles

STRENGTH TRAINING: Trains strength muscles

POWER TRAINING: Trains power muscles

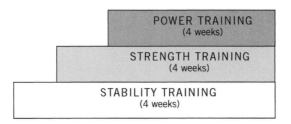

The OPT System

One cycle of the OPT System is 12 weeks (4 weeks of training in each phase: Stability, Strength, and Power). *After completing a full cycle, you will return to the beginning of the OPT System and repeat the entire cycle again—at a higher intensity.*

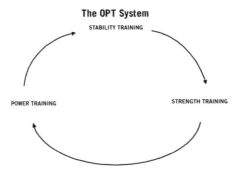

You will repeat the 12-week cycle indefinitely. However, the exercises and intensities will change as you become more conditioned. Why this indefinite cycle through Stability, Strength, and Power Training? Because it's the only way you will get the full benefit of the OPT program—otherwise you will lose the conditioning gains you made during each phase of training. Repeating each phase continuously stimulates the stability, strength, and power muscles, allowing them to reach higher levels of conditioning with each 12-week cycle. On the court, this means performing your personal best time and time again—and staying off the injured list. And your personal best will get better with each 12-week cycle!

Each phase in the OPT System plays a vital role in conditioning your body for *optimum* performance. You may be tempted to skip Stability Training and train only in the Strength or Power Training phases, especially since most basketball conditioning programs focus only on these forms of training. Just remember that it is the *stability* muscles that provide the foundation from which strength and power moves are performed. They are also the key to keeping you injury-free. You will want to recondition them every 12 weeks by cycling back to Stability Training.

Here is how your OPT program will unfold (refer to the chart listed on page 16): Before you begin Stability Training, you will do a Self-Assessment to determine your baseline measurements for total body strength, flexibility, power, speed, agility, and quickness. This Self-Assessment will also help you identify muscle imbalances, another step most basketball conditioning programs mistakenly skip. Why do you need to identify muscle imbalances? As you will learn in Chapter 4, these imbalances occur when a muscle on one side of a joint is tight, causing the muscle on the opposite side to weaken. If your lower back is tight, for example, the muscles of your pelvis and abdomen will be weak. Muscle imbalances like this cause the joint to function improperly and ineffectively. Imbalances affect the motion of other joints in the body, ultimately hindering your performance and setting you up for injury.

You will do a Self-Assessment at the beginning of your OPT program and after completing each phase of training (Stability, Strength, and Power Training).

This is a good point to refer back to what Stephon Marbury wrote in the foreword of this book. "What I like most [about the OPT System] is that everyone's body is treated individually with this program. The exercises are tailored for me—they make me stronger and enable me to work harder so I can build my body to be as efficient as it can be." The initial and check-up Self-Assessments are what make this possible. Remember that there are no good or bad, right or wrong results with the Self-Assessments. They just give you bits of information that allow you to:

1. Identify and correct muscle imbalances.

2. Customize your workouts to fit *your* needs.

3. Assess your progress.

The chart listed below will guide you through your OPT program.

YOUR OPT PROGRAM

Phase	Action	Chapter Reference	Description
	Do initial Self-Assessment	Chapter 6	The Self-Assessment measures flexibility, strength, power, speed, agility, and quickness. It also identifies muscle imbalances, and the Foam Roll and Static Stretching exercises that correct them.
Stability Training	1. Begin Stability Training	Chapter 7	Complete all 4 weeks of Stability Training.
	2. Do Check-up Assessment	Chapter 6	Repeat the Self-Assessment to measure progress and reassess muscle imbalances.
Strength Training	1. Begin Strength Training	Chapter 8	Complete all 4 weeks of Strength Training.
	2. Do Check-up Assessment	Chapter 6	Repeat the Self-Assessment to measure progress and reassess muscle imbalances.
Power Training	1. Begin Power Training	Chapter 9	Complete all 4 weeks of Power Training.

Phase	Action	Chapter Reference	Description
	2. Do Check-up Assessment	Chapter 6	Repeat the Self-Assessment to measure progress and reassess muscle imbalances
	Return to Stability Training		Repeat the entire three-phase OPT System at a higher intensity.

KEY POINT

The OPT program is designed to be followed from beginning to end—just as it is laid out in this book. Skipping any steps is out of the question if you want the exceptional results repeatedly seen by the best NBA players!

TOOLS YOU NEED

Self-Assessment Tools:

1. Athletic tape

2. Chalk

3. Two cones

Workout Preparation Tools:

1. Foam roller

2. Tube

Core Conditioning Tools:

Stability ball

Balance and Plyometric Conditioning Tools:

Box

Speed, Agility, Quickness Tools:

Speed ladder

Resistance Tools:

1. Cable machine

2. Dumbbells

3. Incline bench

4. Seated row machine

5. Medicine ball (5 percent of your weight)

You can purchase these tools by logging on to www.OPT-online.info.

THREE

Set Goals, Play Great!

What do exceptional basketball players, successful business people, and world leaders have in common? They set goals and *reach them* by following a specific plan of action. Each of our athletes at the National Academy of Sports Medicine uses our SMART goal-setting system to set goals for their OPT program. To find out if a goal is SMART, ask the following questions (the goal of "improving your vertical jump" will be used as an example):

> **S = IS YOUR GOAL SPECIFIC?** A goal to increase your vertical jump by *3 inches* is specific.

> **M = IS IT MEASURABLE?** You can measure the progress of your vertical jump with the Vertical Jump Test listed in Chapter 6.

> **A = IS YOUR GOAL ATTAINABLE?** Wanting to increase your vertical jump by 10 inches may not be attainable. A 3-inch increase is a goal you can reach.

R = IS IT RELEVANT TO BASKETBALL? If you want to make your biceps bigger, this goal is neither relevant to basketball nor the *OPT: Basketball* conditioning program. Increasing your vertical jump by 3 inches is very relevant to basketball and this program.

T = CAN YOUR GOAL BE ATTAINED IN THE TIME FRAME YOU HAVE SET? One cycle of your OPT program is twelve weeks. You can achieve a 3-inch increase in your vertical jump in this time frame.

Setting SMART goals forces you to become clear and focused on *WHAT* you want to achieve, *WHY* you want to achieve it, and *HOW* you are going to make it happen. Our experience with NBA players has shown that the more SMART the goals, the more successful you will be at making them come true.

Set your SMART goals now by using the worksheet on the following page.

KEY POINT

Setting *SMART* goals forces you to become clear and focused on *what* you want to achieve, *why* you want to achieve it, and *how* you are going to make it happen.

SMART GOAL SETTING SYSTEM

What-Why-How   **Your Response**

S = What is your *Specific* goal?

M = How will it be *Measured?*

A = Is it *Attainable?*

R = Is it *Relevant* to basketball?

T = Can it be reached in a reasonable
         Time frame?

FOUR

OPT Workout Components

In this chapter, you are going to see a few terms you've probably never seen before, so now is a good time to start thinking out of the box. Don't let these terms intimidate you, though. They are self-explanatory and before long they will be part of your vocabulary.

You need to know about the actual components of your Stability, Strength, and Power workouts before you begin training. You will use the same components throughout each phase, although the exercises and intensities will change to meet the demands of Stability versus Strength versus Power. Each of these components is instrumental in conditioning your body for *optimum* performance and injury prevention on the court, so you don't want to skip any of them. Here are the workout components you will use throughout each phase:

1. WORKOUT PREPARATION: Performed before every workout (Monday through Friday).

2. RESISTANCE TRAINING: Performed on Mondays, Wednesdays, and Fridays.

3. SPEED-AGILITY-QUICKNESS TRAINING: Performed on Tuesdays and Thursdays.

WORKOUT PREPARATION

Would you believe that something as simple as sitting for long periods of time can actually affect how you play on the court—or worse yet, cause an injury? That includes sitting in front of your computer, watching television, or playing video games—basically, anything that requires you to plant your rear in a chair for an extended amount of time.

Sitting a lot can cause muscle imbalances throughout your body. Your calf muscles (the muscles on the back of your lower leg), for example, can become tightened, which causes the muscles on the front of your lower leg (your shin muscles) to be weak. An imbalance of your lower leg muscles can change the motion of your ankle, knee, hip, and spine. That's because your joints work together like a chain. When a joint is altered, all the other joints in the chain are affected as well.

On the court, that means your stride length, ability to change direction, and explosive power may decrease. What's worse is that you increase your chances of an ankle, knee, or back injury.

Besides sitting, other causes of muscle imbalances include:

• A poor training program
• Shoes that do not fit correctly
• Prior injuries that were not properly rehabilitated

Workout preparation exercises correct muscle imbalances. This is why you will perform them at the beginning of every single one of your workouts. Here are a few more benefits these exercises will give you:

- An increase in your range of motion, which is particularly helpful when stealing the ball and blocking passes and shots.

- A decrease in muscle soreness, which allows you to be more limber, flexible, and agile on the court.

- An improvement in posture, which enables you to make the most of your height on the court.

- An increase in strength and power, which improves your ability to post up another player, lay-up, or dunk.

Now that you know how workout preparation will change your game, let's review the six different types of exercise that are part of it:

1. Foam Roll exercises

2. Static Stretching exercises

3. Dynamic Warm-up exercises

4. Core exercises

5. Balance exercises

6. Plyometric exercises

Keep in mind that each of these exercises builds upon the next, so they must always be done in the order listed above. You will perform these exercises five days a week, Monday through Friday, before every single workout.

Foam Roll Exercises

When your muscles are not conditioned properly, your body may substitute a less than effective muscle to do a movement that another muscle is more specifically designed to perform. Take running, for example: when your muscles are properly conditioned, the butt muscles have the primary responsibility of extending your hips when you run. But if the muscles on the front of your hips are tight, the butt muscles will be weakened and less likely to function effectively. This muscle imbalance causes your body to recruit the next best muscle to extend the hips, the muscles on the back of your thighs (the hamstrings). The result? Your performance will not be optimum and your hamstrings will get overworked, causing knots to build up within them.

These knots are also known as muscle spasms and are very similar to a knot in a rope. They cause the muscle to fatigue very quickly, and also cause tightness that prevents the muscle from working through its full range of motion.

Foam Roll exercises release knots by applying deep pressure on these muscle spasms. Think of it as your daily deep tissue massage. This exercise relaxes the muscle and allows it to be stretched back to its normal length—just like a rope returns to its full length when a knot is untied.

Let's use the calf muscle as an example (see illustration below). Place a foam roll at the far end of your calf, just above the ankle, and roll your calf over it until you find a knot or tender spot. Once you find the knot—and you're guaranteed to find one!—apply pressure on it for at least 20 to 30 seconds. You will continue to roll the length of your calf, stopping at each knot and applying pressure. For more details on the Foam Roll, see Chapter 6.

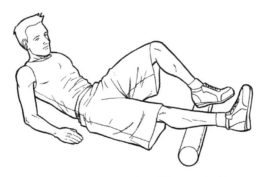

Foam Rolling may get a little uncomfortable, probably even a little painful. But it will be well worth it. When the Dallas Mavericks' head athletic trainer introduced

OPT and Foam Rolling to the team's conditioning program, two players were having chronic tightening of the iliotibial (IT) band on the outer thigh, a problem that can be painful and certainly debilitating. By Foam Rolling their outer thigh before every single workout, Dirk Nowitzki and Jason Terry virtually eliminated their IT problems.

Remember that the results of your Self-Assessment (Chapter 6) will determine the muscles on your body that need to be Foam Rolled.

Static Stretching Exercises

Once the knots are released, the muscle will be ready to be stretched back to its normal length with Static Stretching exercises.

You are probably already familiar with Static Stretching because it is the traditional form of flexibility exercise often used in fitness programs today. Static Stretching elongates a muscle to its original length by passively taking it to its point of tension and holding it there for at least 20 seconds. With the OPT program, you will perform these stretches *after* the knots in the muscles have been released with Foam Roll exercises. This allows the Static Stretching to be more effective.

The results of your Self-Assessment (Chapter 6) will determine the Static Stretching exercises you will perform. An example of these stretches is a Static Hamstring Stretch, which lengthens the muscles on the back of your thigh.

Dynamic Warm-up Exercises

Once the knots have been released and your muscles have been stretched back to their normal length, you are ready for the third component of workout preparation: the Dynamic Warm-up. These active exercises, like the Multiplanar Hops and Lunge Circuit (illustrated below), will strengthen muscle weaknesses and jump-start your body to begin thinking and moving in the range of motion, speed, and direction your workout is going to require.

Lunge Circuit

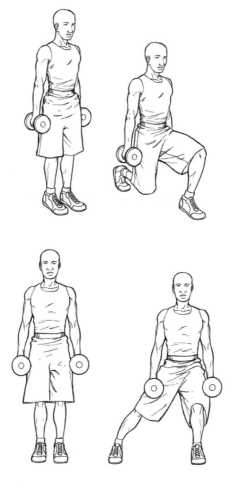

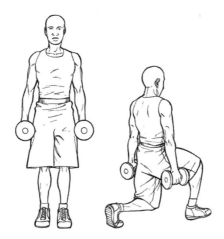

Core Exercises

These days the "core" has become a buzzword in gyms, exercise videos, magazine articles, and conditioning books—and for good reason. It is the place where all movement begins—the foundation of your body that houses your center of gravity. The core consists of your pelvis and spine, and all the muscles that attach to them—basically, everything except your head, arms, and legs.

Why is the core important to you? Research shows that injury usually happens when the core muscles are weak and not effectively contracted prior to movement. In other words, a player with strong and stable core muscles is less likely to have his or her spine rearranged when taking a head-on foul from a charging power forward. The OPT program focuses on stimulating your core muscles before working any other muscles in your body.

Here's an example of a core exercise that you will perform during Stability Training (Chapter 7).

Side Iso-Abs

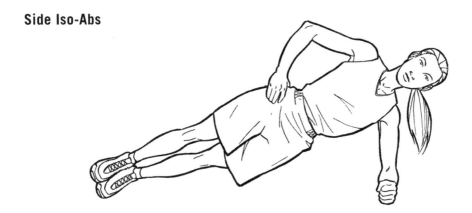

Balance Exercises

Balance is the ability to coordinate your eyes, inner ears (the bones and fluid in your inner ears regulate balance), and muscles at just the right time to generate the speed, direction, and force needed to perform a specific motion. Making a cut, a jump shot, even a free throw requires balance. Most people think that if you're young and active, you don't need to train for balance. This is definitely not so. Balance is a skill that has to be specifically conditioned whether you're a gymnast, dancer, or point guard, which is why it is such an integral part of the OPT program. The ability to balance effectively, in great part, is what separates the exceptional players like Steve Nash from the rest of the pack.

Step-up to Balance is an example of the balance exercises you will use during the Strength Training phase of your OPT program (Chapter 8).

Step-up to Balance

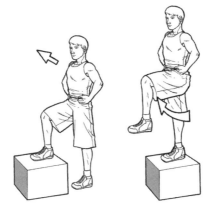

Plyometric Exercises

Plyometric exercises basically use core and balance skills with increased speeds. They involve quick, explosive moves, requiring you to load up (or compress like a spring) and then explode with full force. A rebound, jump shot, and dunk are examples of plyometric moves. Just as with balance, plyometric is a skill that must be acquired. So you will perform plyometric exercises, like a Squat Jump, during workout preparation to train your body to work at the kind of speeds needed to do quick explosive moves on the court. The Squat Jump will be part of your workout preparation exercises during the Strength Training phase (Chapter 8).

Squat Jump

RESISTANCE TRAINING

Many people use the terms Resistance Training and Strength Training interchangeably, though they are not the same thing. Resistance Training is the use of resistance to condition the body for stability, strength, or power. Using resistance to condition your stability muscles is called Resistance *Stability* Training; resistance used to develop your strength muscles is Resistance *Strength* Training; and the use of resistance to condition your power muscles is called Resistance *Power* Training.

You have probably noticed that many training programs consider Resistance Training to be the most important component for conditioning your body. By now, you understand that it is only one of the equally important components of your conditioning program. Resistance Training may actually hinder your performance or set you up for injury if you do not perform workout preparation exercises first.

With OPT, you will use different resistance exercises when training for Stability versus Strength versus Power. For instance, the Standing Dumbbell Shoulder Press is an example of a Resistance *Strength* Training exercise (Chapter 8); the Overhead Medicine Ball Throw is an example of a Resistance *Power* Training exercise (Chapter 9). You will do Resistance Training exercises on Mondays, Wednesdays, and Fridays during Stability, Strength, and Power Training.

**Standing Dumbbell
Shoulder Press**

**Overhead Medicine
Ball Throw**

SPEED-AGILITY-QUICKNESS (SAQ) TRAINING

Speed, agility, and quickness refer to:

1. How fast you can move in one direction (speed).

2. Your ability to start, stop, and change directions quickly, while maintaining proper posture (agility).

3. Your ability to react to a stimulus and change the motion of your body (quickness).

Imagine you're playing offense. The ball gets passed around the perimeter; then your team takes a shot and misses. The other team rebounds the ball and your team transitions to defense by turning (quickness), sprinting (speed), and then changing direction to a backpedal position (agility). You continuously use speed, agility, and quickness while playing basketball so you have to train specifically for them in your workouts.

SAQ exercises improve your footwork skills on the court—for sprinting, shuffling, backpedaling, and changing directions. They also improve your stamina throughout an entire game by conditioning your heart and lungs specifically for basketball. This is one of the reasons Stephon Marbury can play at a very high level of intensity for over 40 minutes per game.

These skills can be learned and improved with training, so you will do SAQ exercises twice a week, on Tuesdays and Thursdays, in all three phases of your OPT program. Here is an example of an SAQ exercise you will be doing in your workouts:

KEY POINT

You will use three components in your Stability, Strength, and Power Training workouts:

1. *Workout Preparation:* performed before every single workout (Monday through Friday).

2. *Resistance Training:* performed on Mondays, Wednesdays, and Fridays.

3. *Speed-Agility-Quickness (SAQ) Training:* performed on Tuesdays and Thursdays.

OPT WORKOUT SCHEDULE

	Stability Training	Strength Training	Power Training
Monday	1. Workout Preparation	1. Workout Preparation	1. Workout Preparation
	2. Resistance Stability Training	2. Resistance Strength Training	2. Resistance Power Training
Tuesday	1. Workout Preparation	1. Workout Preparation	1. Workout Preparation
	2. SAQ Training	2. SAQ Training	2. SAQ Training
Wednesday	1. Workout Preparation	1. Workout Preparation	1. Workout Preparation
	2. Resistance Stability Training	2. Resistance Strength Training	2. Resistance Power Training
Thursday	1. Workout Preparation	1. Workout Preparation	1. Workout Preparation
	2. SAQ Training	2. SAQ Training	2. SAQ Training
Friday	1. Workout Preparation	1. Workout Preparation	1. Workout Preparation
	2. Resistance Stability Training	2. Resistance Strength Training	2. Resistance Power Training
Saturday	DAY OFF	DAY OFF	DAY OFF
Sunday	DAY OFF	DAY OFF	DAY OFF

FIVE

OPT Workout Variables

Each phase of the OPT program—Stability, Strength, and Power—has unique goals for you and your game. So the OPT workout variables—like the amount of weight you lift, and the number of reps and sets you perform, must change within each phase to meet the goals for Stability versus Strength versus Power. Here's a rundown of the workout variables you will be using within each phase of your OPT program.

REPETITION (REP)

A rep is one complete movement of a particular exercise. The number of reps you perform depends on the amount of weight you lift. Each phase of the OPT System requires a different intensity or weight, so the number of reps you perform will change. You will use light weight in Stability Training, which allows you to do a higher number of reps than in other phases. Strength and Power Training require heavier weight, so the number of reps you will do will be limited.

SET

A set is a group of consecutive reps. Because the weight is lighter with Stability Training, you will perform a higher number of reps. This means you will do fewer sets in this phase than in other phases. The opposite happens with Strength and Power Training. The intensity is greater, so you will only be able to do a few reps. This means a higher number of sets in these two phases.

TRAINING INTENSITY (WEIGHT)

Training intensity refers to the amount of effort you exert in an exercise compared to your maximal (max) effort. In other words, it is the amount of weight you will lift. This variable is expressed as a percentage. For example, if your max squat is 200 pounds and your workout requires a training intensity of 70 percent, then you will lift a weight of 140 pounds (70 percent of 200 pounds is 140 pounds) for consecutive reps.

Stability Training requires light weight and Strength Training uses heavier weight. As the *optimum* in Optimum Performance Training, Power Training uses both a low and high intensity. That's because conditioning the power muscles requires that a heavy weight be lifted in a controlled manner immediately followed by a fast, explosive basketball-type movement with light weight, such as a medicine ball.

REP TEMPO

Rep tempo is the speed at which each rep is performed, or the amount of time a muscle is under tension during a repetition. This is the workout variable you may be most tempted to ignore, as most conditioning programs neglect it. But the rep tempo plays a crucial role in differentiating Stability, Strength, and Power Training.

Here's how the rep tempo works in each phase of training. Of the three phases of OPT, Stability Training requires that the muscle be held under tension for the longest period of time, so the rep tempo is slow. Building stronger, larger muscles with Strength Training requires a more moderate rep tempo, while the explosive movements of Power Training demand a very fast rep tempo.

To explain how you will use this workout variable in your OPT program, you have to understand the three different contractions of a repetition. Each of these contractions is equally important and plays a unique role in conditioning your muscles.

1. NEGATIVE CONTRACTION: Lowering the weight.

2. HOLD CONTRACTION: Holding the weight steady, without movement.

3. POSITIVE CONTRACTION: Lifting the weight.

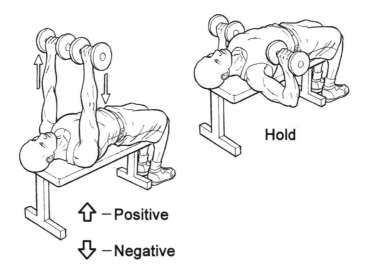

Hold

⇧ —Positive

⇩ —Negative

A rep tempo for Stability Training will be listed in your Stability Training workouts in a three-number sequence such as 4-2-1. Using a Chest Press example, this means:

4 seconds to lower the weight toward your chest;

2 seconds to hold the weight steady, without movement;

1 second to push the weight back up away from your chest.

The rep tempo for Strength Training may be listed in your workouts as 2-0-2. This means it will take you 2 seconds to lower the weight toward your chest and then without pausing, you will take 2 seconds to push the weight up away from your chest.

Power Training uses exercises that simulate actual basketball moves. These quick, explosive movements require you to act with as much speed and control as possible. The rep tempo will be listed in your Power Training workouts as (x-x-x). This means the movement is very fast and explosive and requires you to act without any hesitation or pause, like a rebound.

REST INTERVAL

The time you take to recuperate between sets and/or exercises is called the rest interval. Each exercise that you perform requires energy. The rest interval allows some of that energy to be replenished so you can perform the next set or exercise. Depending on how fit you are, Strength and Power exercises can require up to 2 minutes of rest between sets. In the beginning, you may respond better to longer rest periods until your body adjusts to the demands of your OPT program.

Here is an outline of the workout variables you will use in your OPT program.

OPT SYSTEM WORKOUT VARIABLES

OPT Phase	Reps	Sets	Intensity	Rep Tempo	Rest Interval
Stability Training	High 12–15	Low 2–3	60–70% Max effort	Slow 4–2–1	30–60 seconds
Strength Training	Moderate 8–12	Moderate 2–4	70–80% Max effort	Moderate 3–2–1 to 2–0–2	30–90 seconds
Power Training	**Strength Set** Low 1–5	High 3–5	**Strength Set** 80–90%	**Strength Set** 2–0–2	30 seconds– 2 min
	Power Set High 8–10		**Power Set** 2–10% Body weight	**Power Set** Explosive (x–x–x)	

Other workout variables include how often you will work out and the amount of time it will take to do each workout. These variables are called training frequency and training duration.

TRAINING FREQUENCY

Training frequency refers to the number of training sessions you will perform within a week. You will work out five days a week throughout all three phases of your OPT program. Your workouts during each phase of training will be broken down like this:

STABILITY TRAINING

1. Workout Preparation (M–F)

2. Resistance Stability Training (M, W, F)

3. SAQ Training (T, Th)

↓

STRENGTH TRAINING

1. Workout Preparation (M–F)

2. Resistance Strength Training (M, W, F)

3. SAQ Training (T, Th)

↓

POWER TRAINING

1. Workout Preparation (M–F)

2. Resistance Power Training (M, W, F)

3. SAQ Training (T, Th)

Of course, the workout preparation, Resistance Training, and Speed-Agility-Quickness exercises will differ from one phase to the next. In other words, the exercises and intensities performed during Stability Training will condition the stability muscles. Those performed during Strength Training will focus specifically on conditioning the strength muscles; and the Power Training exercises and intensities will emphasize the development of power muscles.

TRAINING DURATION

Training duration refers to two components:

1. How long it takes to do your workout.

2. The number of weeks spent in one phase.

Your OPT workouts will take between 60 and 90 minutes. You will train within each phase of the OPT System for 4 weeks.

KEY POINT

The workout variables in the OPT system will lead you to exceptional results because they are designed to fully develop your stability, strength, and power muscles for basketball.

Part II
THE WORKOUT

SIX

Self-Assessment

One of the most important concepts you will take away from this book is how deeply your physical activity is affected by muscle imbalances. That's why the first step of your OPT program is to identify muscle imbalances in your body by taking the Overhead and Single-Leg Squat tests described in this chapter. The results of these two assessments will be used to customize the Foam Roll and Static Stretching exercises you will use in your workouts to correct these imbalances.

Jumping, sprinting, and moving quickly in every direction are all constants in basketball, making speed, agility, quickness, and power essential components of the game. These skills can fortunately be learned and honed with the proper conditioning program, but they must first be assessed to identify opportunities for improvement. You will do this with the Sharks Skill, Vertical Jump, and LEFT tests described in this chapter. These assessments, along with the Overhead and Single-Leg Squat tests, are great tools for determining your baseline capabilities and checking the progress you make in each phase of training. That's why you will perform them when you first begin the OPT program and then again at the end of each 4-week phase. Don't forget to use the forms in this chapter to chart your progress. If you follow the OPT program as outlined in this book, you are going to be absolutely amazed by your reassessment results!

OVERHEAD AND SINGLE-LEG SQUAT TESTS

Each muscle has an opposing muscle with an opposing movement. So if the muscles on one side of a joint are tightened, the muscles on the other side will be lengthened or weakened. An imbalance of the hip muscles is a good example to use since it is so common in our society. If the muscles on the front of your hips (the hip flexors) are tight, the opposing muscles that extend the hip (the butt muscles) will be weak. Why is this so significant? As mentioned earlier, the joints in your body function like a chain; this means an imbalance of one joint will alter the movement of other joints in your body. So the hip imbalance mentioned above could affect not only the motion of your hip joint, but possibly even your ankle, knee, shoulder, and neck!

Most muscle imbalances are caused by everyday movements like sitting, poor posture, and improper training programs. Even old injuries that were not properly rehabilitated and shoes that do not fit correctly can cause muscle imbalances. What do these imbalances have to do with conditioning for basketball? Everything! Altered joint motion affects the way you run, jump, shoot, balance, and change directions. Do you use these moves in basketball? You bet!

That's why muscle imbalances typically mean less court play and more bench time due to poor performance and injuries. In fact, research shows that the risk of injury to the anterior cruciate ligament (ACL), which is a common and debilitating knee injury in basketball, increases 70 to 80 percent for athletes with altered knee motion due to muscle imbalance. The athletes training with the OPT System have decreased ACL and other injuries by correcting and preventing these imbalances. See the illustration below for the muscle imbalances commonly found in basketball players.

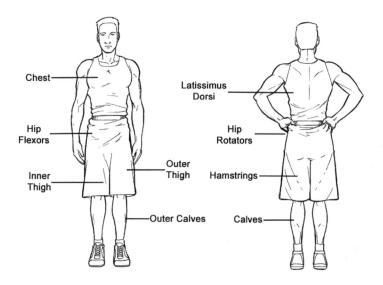

The Overhead and Single-Leg Squat tests will identify your muscle imbalances and help you customize the Foam Roll and Static Stretching exercises that will correct them. This is a good time to remind you that Foam Roll exercises release the knots in your tight muscles by applying deep pressure on them, and Static Stretching exercises stretch the muscles back to their normal length after the knots have been released.

Let's get started with your Overhead and Single-Leg Squat Assessments.

OVERHEAD SQUAT ASSESSMENT

This test identifies your muscle imbalances and measures your total body flexibility, strength, balance, and control. You will perform an Overhead Squat in front of a full-length mirror and then answer a series of seven questions regarding the movement of your upper and lower body during the squat. The responses to these questions will help identify your muscle imbalances.

Instructions

1. Stand 3 feet away from a full-length mirror with feet shoulder-width apart and toes pointing straight ahead.

2. Extend your arms directly overhead as if reaching for the sky.

3. Keep your arms overhead and squat three times—as if squatting into a chair.

4. Hold the last squat and look into the mirror to answer the following questions. Record your answers (Yes/No) in the chart on page 58:

Did your feet turn out like in the picture below?

Did your feet flatten like in the picture below?

Did your knees move in toward each other like in the picture below?

Did your knees move out from each other like in the picture below?

5. Standing sideways in front of the mirror, repeat instruction steps 1 to 4 listed on page 54, then answer the questions below:

Did your back arch like in the picture below?

Did your upper body lean forward like in the picture below?

Did your arms move forward like in the picture below?

OVERHEAD AND SINGLE-LEG

Observation

(Yes or No)

DATE

Feet Turn Out?

Feet Flatten?

Knees Move In?

Knees Move Out?

Back Arch?

Upper Body Leans Forward?

Arms Move Forward?

Knee Move In?

Upper Body Shifts to One Side?

You can download this form by going to www.OPT-online.info.

Use the form below to chart your progress with the Overhead Squat Test and Single-Leg Squat Test (described on page 61) throughout all three phases of the OPT program. The initial assessment is listed as "Before Stability Training," and the check-up assessments performed at the end of each phase are listed as "After Stability Training," "After Strength Training," and "After Power Training."

The shaded blocks on the chart indicate those observations that do not apply to the particular test.

SQUAT ASSESSMENT RESULTS

Overhead Squat   **Single-Leg Squat**

Before Stability Training	After Stability Training	After Strength Training	After Power Training	Before Stability Training	After Stability Training	After Strength Training	After Power Training
				L R	L R	L R	L R

If you answered "yes" to any of the questions for the Overhead Squat Test, refer to the chart below to identify the Foam Roll and Static Stretching exercises you will do before every single workout to correct your imbalances.

OVERHEAD SQUAT ASSESSMENT RESULTS

Checkpoint	Observation	Tight Muscles	Foam Roll	Static Stretching
Foot	Turns Out	Calves	Calves	Calves
Foot	Flattens	Outer Calves	Outer Calves	Calves
Knees	Move In	Inner Thighs	Inner Thighs Outer Thighs	Inner Thighs
Knees	Move Out	Hip Rotators, Hamstrings	Hip Rotators	Hip Rotators, Hamstrings
Back	Arches	Hip Flexors	Outer Thighs, Hip Flexors	Hip Flexors
Upper Body	Leans Forward	Calves, Hip Flexors	Calves	Calves, Hip Flexors
Arms	Move Forward	Lats, Chest	Lats, Upper Back	Lats, Chest

You can download this form by going to www.OPT-online.info.

To read the chart correctly, simply read horizontally across the columns beginning on the left with the observations you found when you did the assessments. For example, if you found that your feet turned out, then you know that your calf muscles are tight and need both Foam Roll and Static Stretching exercises.

SINGLE-LEG SQUAT ASSESSMENT

This test identifies your muscle imbalances and assesses total body flexibility, strength, balance, and control on a single leg. Once again, you will stand in front of a full-length mirror to perform the squat. You will then answer two questions regarding the movement of your upper and lower body during the squat. The responses to these questions will help identify your muscle imbalances.

Instructions:

1. Stand 3 feet away from a full-length mirror with toes pointing straight ahead.

2. Stand on your right leg with left leg lifted directly beside it (do not let legs touch each other). Hands on hips.

3. Squat as if squatting into a chair, keeping your hands on your hips.

4. Squat three times and hold the last one to answer the following questions (record your answers on the chart on page 58):

Did your knee move in like in the picture below?

Did your upper body shift to one side like in the picture below?

5. Repeat Steps 1 through 4 standing on left leg with right leg lifted directly beside it (do not let legs touch each other).

If you answered "yes" to either of the above questions, refer to the following chart to identify the Foam Roll and Static Stretching exercises that you will do before every single workout to correct your imbalances.

SINGLE-LEG SQUAT ASSESSMENT RESULTS

Checkpoint	Observation	Tight Muscles	Foam Roll	Static Stretching
Knee	Moves In	Inner Thighs	Inner Thighs, Outer Thighs	Inner Thighs, Hip Flexors
Upper Body	Shifts to Side	Inner Thighs, Hip Rotators	Inner Thighs, Hip Rotators	Inner Thighs, Hip Rotators

You can download this form by going to www.OPT-online.info.

Don't be alarmed if you have several or all of the observations listed in both of the charts above. This is common. These tests simply indicate opportunities to enhance your performance and prevent injury by identifying and correcting muscle imbalances. The following pages illustrate and describe how to perform the Foam Roll and Static Stretching exercises listed on the charts. Remember, you don't have to do all of these exercises illustrated on the following pages, just the ones your Self-Assessment indicates.

Answering "no" to all of the Overhead and Single-Leg Squat assessment questions means you do not demonstrate any significant muscle imbalances in your upper or lower body. You will still perform preventive Foam Roll exercises for your calves and outer thighs, and Static Stretching exercises for your calves and hip flexors before every single workout. These exercises will lengthen the muscles and prepare them for the Dynamic Warm-up. They are illustrated in the following pages.

PROPER POSTURE POSITION

"Proper posture position" is a phrase you will see mentioned repeatedly in the exercises throughout this book. Proper posture allows your muscles and joints to work together most effectively and will also help you make the most of your height. It includes these four main points:

1. DRAW IN YOUR ABDOMINALS: The best way to describe this is to imagine drawing in your belly button so you can squeeze into a tight pair of pants.

2. LIFT YOUR CHEST: Squeeze your shoulder blades together and lift your chest.

3. LOWER YOUR SHOULDERS: Avoid raising your shoulders toward your ears; keep them relaxed.

4. TUCK YOUR CHIN: Your earlobes should be in line with your shoulders and your shoulders in line with your hips. If you see that your earlobes are positioned in front of your shoulders, tuck your chin to avoid straining your neck muscles.

5. POINT FEET STRAIGHT AHEAD: Avoid letting your feet point in or out.

6. ALIGN YOUR KNEES AND TOES: Your knees should align over your second and third toes when squatting.

FOAM ROLL FOR CALVES

1. Place foam roll under mid-calf.

2. Cross left leg over right leg to increase pressure (optional).

3. Slowly roll calf area to find most tender spot.

4. Apply pressure on tender spot for 30 seconds.

5. Progress to next tender spot and hold again.

6. Repeat on opposite leg.

Tip

Maintain proper posture position throughout the entire exercise.

FOAM ROLL FOR OUTER CALVES

1. Place foam roll under outer part of calf.

2. Cross left leg over right leg to increase pressure (optional).

3. Slowly roll calf area to find most tender spot.

4. Apply pressure on tender spot and hold for 30 seconds.

5. Progress to next tender spot and hold again.

6. Repeat on opposite leg.

Tip

Maintain proper posture position throughout the entire exercise.

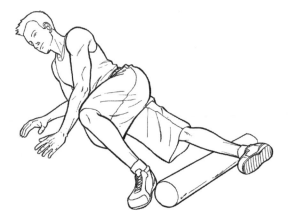

FOAM ROLL FOR OUTER THIGH

1. Lie with foam roll under side and slightly in front of hip.

2. Cross top leg over lower leg, with foot touching floor and bottom leg raised slightly off floor.

3. Maintain proper head alignment (ears in line with shoulders).

4. Slowly roll from upper portion of outer thigh, slightly in front of hip joint, to knee.

5. Apply pressure on tender spot for 30 seconds.

6. Progress to next tender spot and hold again.

7. Repeat on opposite leg.

Tip

Maintain proper posture position throughout the entire exercise.

FOAM ROLL FOR INNER THIGH

1. Lie on stomach with one thigh extended slightly out to side and knee bent.

2. Place foam roll in groin region, under upper thigh.

3. Slowly roll inner thigh area to find most tender spot.

4. Apply pressure on tender spot for 30 seconds.

5. Progress to next tender spot and hold again.

6. Repeat on opposite leg.

Tip

Maintain proper posture position throughout the entire exercise.

FOAM ROLL FOR HIP ROTATORS

1. Sit with foam roll positioned on back of hip.

2. Cross one foot to opposite knee (optional).

3. Lean into hip of crossed leg.

4. Slowly roll on back of hip area to find most tender spot.

5. Apply pressure on tender spot for 30 seconds.

6. Progress to next tender spot and hold again.

7. Repeat on opposite leg.

Tip

Maintain proper posture position throughout the entire exercise.

FOAM ROLL FOR HIP FLEXORS

1. Sit with foam roll positioned on front of hip.
2. Cross top leg over lower leg, with top foot touching floor and bottom leg raised off floor.
3. Lean into hip of extended leg.
4. Slowly roll on front of hip area to find most tender spot.
5. Apply pressure on tender spot for 30 seconds.
6. Progress to next tender spot and hold again.
7. Repeat on opposite leg.

Tip

Maintain proper posture position throughout the entire exercise.

FOAM ROLL FOR UPPER BACK

1. Sit on floor with foam roll placed behind back.

2. Cross arms to opposite shoulders.

3. Raise hips off floor.

4. Slowly move back and forth to find most tender spot.

5. Apply pressure on tender spot for 30 seconds.

6. Progress to next tender spot and hold again.

Tip

Maintain proper posture position throughout the entire exercise.

FOAM ROLL FOR LATISSIMUS DORSI (LATS)

1. Lie on one side with arm closest to floor extended overhead and thumb pointing up.

2. Place foam roll in area under shoulder.

3. Slowly move back and forth to find most tender spot.

4. Apply pressure on tender spot for 30 seconds.

5. Progress to next tender spot and hold again.

6. Repeat on opposite side.

Tip

Maintain proper posture position throughout the entire exercise.

STATIC CALF STRETCH

1. Stand facing a wall or sturdy object in a staggered stance (one leg forward toward wall and other leg extended back).

2. Place hands on wall at shoulder level and wider than shoulder-width apart.

3. Bend arms to move chest toward wall.

4. Stop movement when slight tension is felt in back of lower leg.

5. Hold for 30 seconds.

6. Switch sides and repeat.

Tips

- Maintain proper posture position throughout the entire exercise.

- Keep rear foot flat and pointed straight ahead (do not allow rear foot to turn out).

- Maintain a straight line from earlobe to shoulder to hip to heel of back foot when shifting toward wall (avoid bending at waist or arching back).

STATIC HAMSTRING STRETCH (BACK OF THIGH)

1. Lie on floor with legs flat.

2. Flex hip and knee of one leg, creating 90-degree angles in both joints.

3. With hands supporting leg, slowly extend knee until tension is felt.

4. Hold for 30 seconds.

5. Switch sides and repeat.

Tip

- Maintain proper posture position throughout the entire exercise.

- Avoid lifting hips off floor when performing stretch.

STATIC INNER THIGH STRETCH

1. Stand with feet straight and legs slightly wider than shoulder-width apart.

2. Draw in belly button away from belt line.

3. Slowly move sideways by bending one leg and keeping opposite leg straight. Continue until a stretch in groin area of straight leg is felt.

4. Hold for 30 seconds.

5. Switch sides and repeat.

Tip

Maintain proper posture position throughout the entire exercise.

STATIC KNEELING HIP FLEXOR STRETCH

1. Kneel on back leg with front leg bent at a 90-degree angle.

2. Squeeze butt muscles and tilt pelvis so shoulder, hip, and back knee are in alignment.

3. Slowly shift body forward.

4. Raise your arm—same side as rear leg—over your head until the upper arm is by your ear. Reach to opposite side until stretch is felt in front of pelvis.

5. Maintain this position and slowly rotate torso back until you are looking under your arm.

6. Hold for 30 seconds.

7. Switch sides and repeat.

Tips

- Maintain proper posture position throughout the entire exercise.
- Point the toes of the rear foot inward to accentuate the stretch.

STATIC HIP ROTATOR STRETCH

1. Lie on back with foot placed over opposite thigh.

2. Place hand on knee and slowly pull to opposite shoulder until stretch is felt in back of hip.

3. Hold for 30 seconds.

4. Switch sides and repeat.

Tip

Maintain proper posture position throughout the entire exercise.

STATIC LAT STRETCH

1. Kneel in front of a stability ball.

2. Place one arm on ball (thumb pointed up) and other hand on ground.

3. Reach arm forward to feel stretch along side of torso into lower back.

4. Attempt to round back by touching butt to heels.

5. Hold for 30 seconds.

6. Switch sides and repeat.

Tip

Maintain proper posture position throughout the entire exercise.

STATIC CHEST STRETCH

1. Stand in a door frame with one arm placed on frame, shoulder and elbow bent 90 degrees.

2. Slowly rotate upper body away from arm on door frame until a slight stretch is felt in chest and front shoulder area.

3. Hold for 30 seconds.

4. Switch sides and repeat.

Tip

Maintain proper posture position throughout the entire exercise.

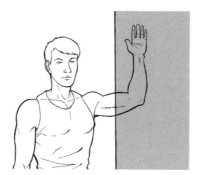

SHARKS SKILL TEST

This test, named after its creators Marc *Sherry* and Dr. Mike *Clark* (Sherry and Clark: *Shark*), measures foot quickness by assessing your ability to hop in various directions on one foot. You will refer to the illustration below to perform this assessment.

Instructions

1. Begin in the center box (X) on one leg with hands on your hips.

2. Hop to each corresponding box (1–8), returning to the center box between each hop. So you will hop to box 1, then back to center box X; box 2 then back to box X, and so on, using the same leg.

3. Measure the total time it takes you to complete the pattern on both the right and left leg. Using a digital stopwatch, record in seconds to the nearest hundredth of a second, in the chart on page 82.

4. Penalty: Add 10 seconds to your total time each time any of the following occur:

- Nonhopping leg touches the ground.

- Hands come off your hips.

- Foot goes into the wrong square.

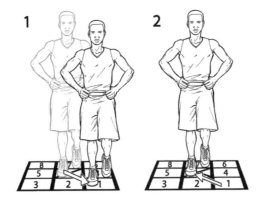

VERTICAL JUMP TEST

This test assesses your vertical jump on two legs and one leg.

Instructions

1. Stand close to wall with feet shoulder-width apart.

2. Place chalk in hand.

3. Keeping your feet on the ground, reach as high as possible with one hand and place a mark on the wall at that point.

4. Holding the piece of chalk, jump as high as possible on both legs. Mark the wall with chalk at the highest point above the original mark that you can reach with one hand while jumping.

5. Perform three jumps and record the highest to the nearest half inch on the chart on page 83.

6. The height of your vertical jump is the difference between the mark made while standing and the mark made while jumping.

7. Repeat steps 1 through 5 standing on your right leg, reaching as high as possible with your left hand.

8. Repeat steps 1 through 5, standing on your left leg, reaching as high as possible with your right hand.

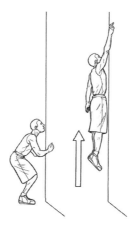

LEFT (LOWER EXTREMITY FUNCTIONAL TEST)

This test measures your speed, agility, quickness, and your ability to change direction. It encompasses the majority of the lower body movements that occur in basketball.

Instructions

1. Place two cones or markers 10 yards from each other.

2. Start at point A and progress as follows:

    a. Sprint to point B

    b. Backpedal to point A

    c. Side shuffle to point B

    d. Side shuffle to point A

    e. Crossover step* to point B

    f. Crossover step* to point A

    g. Sprint to point B

SHARKS SKILL, VERTICAL JUMP,

Sharks Skill

	Before Stability Training	After Stability Training	After Strength Training	After Power Training
Date				
Results (Time)				

You can download this form by going to www.OPT-online.info.

*Crossover step = side step to right, then cross left leg over right, side step to right again, then cross left leg behind right. Repeat all the way to point B, then change direction and repeat with opposite leg motion to point A.

3. Stop the timer when you cross an imaginary line at end of point B. Measure time in seconds to the nearest tenth of a second and record on the chart below.

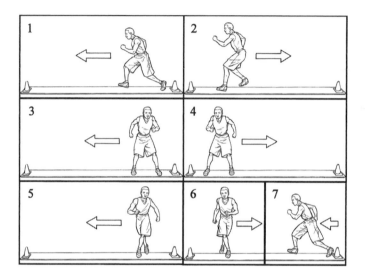

AND LEFT TESTS RESULTS

Vertical Jump   **LEFT**

Before Stability Training	After Stability Training	After Strength Training	After Power Training	Before Stability Training	After Stability Training	After Strength Training	After Power Training

The initial assessment is referred to as "Before Stability Training" in the chart above, and the check-up assessments conducted at the end of each phase are referred to as "After Stability Training," "After Strength Training," and "After Power Training."

SEVEN

Stability Training

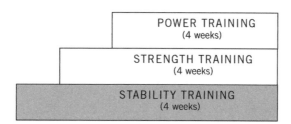

The OPT System

Now that you have identified your muscle imbalances and have assessed your speed, agility, quickness, strength, and power, you are ready to begin training. Stability Training is the foundation of your OPT program because it trains some of the most fundamental muscles of your body—the stability muscles. These deep, supportive muscles are sometimes referred to as the "invisible muscles" because you can't see them. They protect your joints from injury, give you endurance to hold defensive positions for extended periods of time and provide the platform from which strength and power movements are performed. Without conditioned stability muscles, you could never be strong enough to fight through the pick or powerful enough to rise above a defender to shoot a jumper.

Stability Training focuses specifically on conditioning your stability muscles for basketball moves. This chapter will review the components of your Stability Training workouts so that you can progress through the 4 weeks of Stability Training that are detailed in the last few pages of this chapter. You will train 5 days a week (Monday through Friday) in this phase with the following workout components:

STABILITY TRAINING: WORKOUT COMPONENTS

See Chapter 4 for detailed definitions.

1. WORKOUT PREPARATION: Performed before every workout (Monday through Friday).

2. RESISTANCE STABILITY TRAINING: Performed on Mondays, Wednesdays, and Fridays.

3. SPEED-AGILITY-QUICKNESS TRAINING: Performed on Tuesdays and Thursdays.

WORKOUT PREPARATION

The purpose of workout preparation is just as the name implies, *to prepare your body to work out*. Workout preparation corrects muscle imbalances and actively stretches your muscles though a full range of motion. There are six components to workout preparation: Foam Roll, Static Stretching, Dynamic Warm-up, Core, Balance, and Plyometric.

Foam Roll and Static Stretching Exercises

The Overhead and Single-Leg Squat Assessments (Chapter 6) will determine if you have muscle imbalances. The assessment questions and chart in Chapter 6 will identify your imbalances and direct you to the Foam Roll and Static Stretching exercises that will correct them. You will perform these exercises at the beginning of every single workout (5 days a week) throughout each week of Stability Training.

Dynamic Warm-up Exercises

Once the knots in your muscles have been released and your muscles have been stretched back to their normal length, you are ready for the third part of workout preparation: the Dynamic Warm-up. This technique actively moves your muscles through their full range of motion, preparing and training your body to work in the range, speed, and direction that the rest of your workout will require. You will perform the same Dynamic Warm-up exercises at the beginning of every single workout throughout all three phases of training.

Here are the Dynamic Warm-up exercises you will perform in the Stability, Strength, and Power Training phases.

TUBE WALKING: SIDE TO SIDE

1. Stand with feet hip-width apart, knees slightly bent, and feet straight ahead.

2. Place tubing around ankles.

3. Keep feet and knees pointing straight ahead and take small steps sideways.

4. Repeat in opposite direction.

Tips

- Maintain proper posture position throughout the entire exercise.

- Do not allow knees to cave in or feet to turn out.

LUNGE CIRCUIT

1. Stand with feet straight ahead and shoulder-width apart.

2. Hold dumbbell in each hand, palms facing side of body.

3. Lunge forward, landing on heel of lunge foot, foot straight ahead, knee bent at 90-degree angle. Back leg is also bent at 90-degree angle, heel lifted off floor.

4. Push off heel of front foot onto back leg.

5. Return to start position.

6. Lunge sideways; stabilize with lunge foot straight ahead, knee bent and directly over second and third toes; opposite leg straight with foot flat on ground.

7. Push off bent leg to return to start position.

8. Turn and lunge by opening hips and stepping back in 45-degree angle, pivoting on back foot.

9. Stabilize with front foot straight ahead, knee bent at 90-degree angle and directly over second and third toes; opposite leg bent at 90-degree angle, heel of back foot off ground.

10. Push off front foot to return to start position.

Tips

• Maintain proper posture position throughout the entire exercise.

• Avoid using momentum in this exercise. Perform the lunges with control.

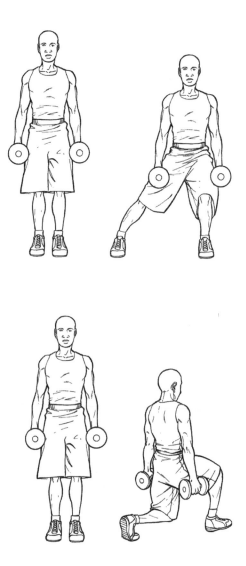

SINGLE-LEG SQUAT TOUCHDOWN

1. Stand with feet straight ahead and hip-width apart.

2. Stand in proper posture position (abdominals drawn in, chest lifted, shoulders down, chin tucked) and place hands on hips.

3. Squeeze butt muscles, balance on one leg, and lift other directly beside it.

4. Keep shoulders and hips level.

5. Slowly squat, bending hip and knee.

6. Reach opposite hand toward balance foot and hold for 2 seconds.

7. Pushing through heel, slowly return to start position.

8. Repeat as instructed.

9. Switch legs and repeat.

Tip

Maintain proper posture position throughout the entire exercise.

SINGLE-LEG MULTIPLANAR HOPS

1. Stand with feet straight ahead and shoulder-width apart.

2. Squeeze butt muscles, balance on right leg and lift left leg directly beside it, knee in line with toe.

3. Hop forward, landing on left foot. Stabilize and hold for 2 to 4 seconds.

4. Hop backward to start position, landing on right foot. Stabilize and hold for 2 to 4 seconds.

5. Switch legs and repeat.

6. Hop sideways, landing on left foot. Stabilize and hold for 2 to 4 seconds.

7. Hop sideways to start position, landing on right foot. Stabilize and hold for 2 to 4 seconds.

8. Hop turning back at 45-degree angle, landing on left foot. Stabilize and hold for 2 to 4 seconds.

9. Hop turning forward at 45-degree angle, landing on right foot to return to start position. Stabilize and hold for 2 to 4 seconds.

10. Switch legs and repeat.

11. Repeat steps 1 through 10 above as instructed.

Tips

- Maintain proper posture position throughout the entire exercise.

- Avoid using momentum in this exercise. Perform the hops with control.

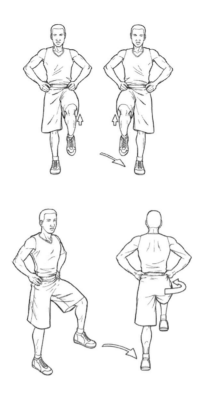

Core Exercises

It is important to remind you here that the core is the place where all movement begins. It houses your body's center of gravity and consists of your pelvis, spine, and all
the muscles that attach to them—basically, everything except your head, arms, and
legs.

Your core muscles have two responsibilities. They stabilize and move the spine.
When movement occurs, your stability muscles contract to hold your pelvis and spine
in place. Most conditioning programs focus only on core movement with exercises like
abdominal crunches and neglect to train core stability. Will this cause a problem?
Eventually, yes. When your movement muscles are proportionately stronger than your

stability muscles, injury may occur. That's why your core should be trained for both stability and strength.

Stability Training trains your core *stability* muscles. Strength Training trains your core *strength* muscles, and Power Training your core *power* muscles. You will notice the exercises that condition the core stability muscles use little motion throughout the pelvis and spine.

Here are the core stability exercises you will do during Stability Training.

SIDE ISO-ABS

1. Lie on one side with feet and legs stacked on top of each other, forearm on ground and elbow under shoulder.

2. Draw in belly button and squeeze butt muscles.

3. Lift hips and legs off ground until body forms a straight line from head to toe, resting on forearm and feet.

4. Hold for 2 seconds.

5. Slowly lower body to ground.

6. Repeat as instructed.

Tip

Maintain proper posture position throughout the entire exercise.

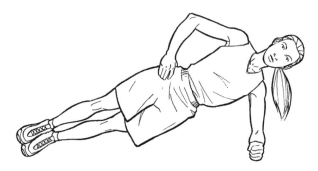

FLOOR BRIDGE WITH ALTERNATE LEG

1. Lie on back with knees bent, feet flat and shoulder-width apart.

2. Keeping one foot flat on floor, slightly lift other foot off floor.

3. Place arms to side.

4. Draw in belly button, squeeze butt muscles, and lift pelvis off floor until knees, hips, and shoulders are in line, pushing through heels.

5. Slowly extend elevated knee, completely straightening leg.

6. Hold for 2 seconds.

7. Bend knee, placing both feet flat on floor, and slowly lower pelvis to start position.

8. Repeat as instructed and then switch legs.

Tip

Maintain proper posture position throughout the entire exercise.

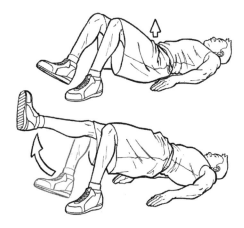

ALL FOURS: ARM OPPOSITE LEG

1. Position yourself on all fours.

2. Draw in belly button and squeeze butt muscles.

3. Slowly raise arm with thumb up and extend opposite leg behind; keep back flat.

4. Keep arm and leg straight, lifting both until in line with body.

5. Hold for 2 seconds; slowly return arm and leg to floor.

6. Repeat, alternating sides, as instructed.

Tip

Maintain proper posture position throughout the entire exercise.

Balance Exercises

Balance exercises condition your body to contract the right muscles at the right time. You use balance for obvious reasons like standing on one leg, but also for challenging movements like a reverse lay-up or fall-away jumper. Before you progress to conditioning balance in motion, you have to first condition your ability to balance in place. You will do this in Stability Training with the Single-Leg Balance Reach. This exercise, illustrated below, will prepare you for the balance-in-motion exercises you will perform in Strength Training.

SINGLE-LEG BALANCE REACH

1. Stand with feet straight ahead and hip-width apart.

2. Get into proper posture position (abdominals drawn in, chest lifted, shoulders down, chin tucked).

3. Squeeze butt muscles and balance on one leg. Lift other leg directly beside it.

4. Point lifted leg to front of body.

5. Hold for 2 seconds then slowly return to start.

6. Point lifted leg to side of body.

7. Hold for 2 seconds then slowly return to start position.

8. Switch legs and repeat as instructed.

Tips

- Maintain proper posture position throughout the entire exercise.
- Keep hips and shoulders level.

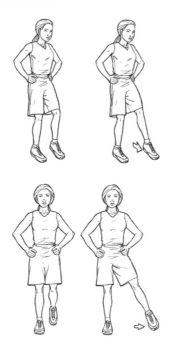

Plyometric Exercises

Plyometrics is another one of those unusual conditioning words that will soon become part of your vocabulary. Plyometric exercises involve quick, explosive movements like a spring unloading. Off the top of your head, you can probably think of a dozen or so plyometric moves you use on the court, like shot blocking or a lay-up. They typically involve jumping and landing. In Stability Training, you will focus on the landing or stability portion of a plyometric move with the Box Jump-up exercise illustrated below.

BOX JUMP-UP AND HOLD

1. Stand in front of a box or platform (6 to 18 inches high) with feet straight ahead and shoulder-width apart.

2. Get into proper posture position (abdominals drawn in, chest lifted, shoulders down, chin tucked).

3. Squeeze butt muscles.

4. Using arms and legs, jump up and land on top of box with both feet (feet pointed straight ahead and knees directly in line with toes).

5. Stabilize for 2 to 4 seconds.

6. Step off box and return to start.

7. Repeat as instructed.

Tip

Maintain proper posture position throughout the entire exercise.

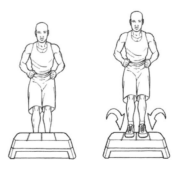

RESISTANCE STABILITY TRAINING

You will use resistance to train your stability, strength, and power muscles in the OPT program. Your focus in Stability Training will be on your *stability* muscles. The goal for Resistance Training in this phase is to improve your ability to hold your pelvis and spine in place during movement, so your arms and legs can work more efficiently on the court. Think about these basic moves: dribbling, shooting, passing, and guarding. They all require the spine and pelvis to be locked into place or stabilized so that your arms and legs can effectively execute the desired movement. Imagine what would happen if your spine wasn't stabilized. Instead of being quick, fluid, and precise on the court, you would be clumsy, jerky, and inconsistent in your play.

Resistance Stability Training requires high reps, few sets, low intensity, and a slow rep tempo. These workout variables are listed below and are also detailed in your Stability Training workouts at the end of this chapter.

RESISTANCE STABILITY WORKOUT VARIABLES

Reps	Sets	Intensity	Rep Tempo	Rest Interval
12 to 15	2 to 3	60 to 70% Max Effort	Slow 4–2–1	About 30 seconds between supersets
				About 60 seconds between circuits

See Chapter 5 for detailed definitions of workout variables.

Sets in these workouts are designed to be performed in a circuit training format. This means you will perform the exercises one right after the other, with approximately 30 seconds of rest in between. If you feel you have recovered before 30 seconds, you can continue with your next exercise. After the last exercise, you will rest for approximately 60 seconds and then repeat the series of exercises again as directed by the number of sets listed.

Using the workout variables listed above, you will perform the following Resistance Stability Training exercises on Monday, Wednesday, and Friday throughout each week of Stability Training.

STAGGERED-STANCE CABLE CHEST PRESS

1. Stand with back to weight stack, feet straight ahead and in a staggered-stance (back leg straight, front leg bent).
2. Hold a cable in each hand at chest level (palms face down), elbows bent and slightly below shoulder level.
3. Press both cables forward and together, fully extending arms and squeezing chest muscles.
4. Slowly return hands to start position.

Tips

- Maintain proper posture position throughout the entire exercise.
- Do not allow head to jut forward or shoulders to rise toward ears.

STANDING CABLE ROW

1. Stand facing a cable machine with feet straight ahead and shoulder-width apart.

2. Hold cables with palms facing inward and arms extended at chest level.

3. With knees and hips slightly bent, row by bringing thumbs toward armpits, squeezing shoulder blades together.

4. Hold, then return to start position.

5. Repeat as instructed.

Tips

- Maintain proper posture position throughout the entire exercise.

- Do not allow head to jut forward or shoulders to rise toward ears.

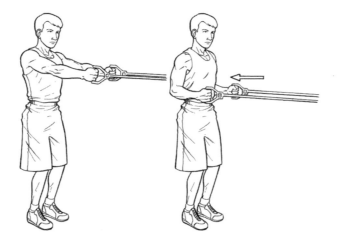

STANDING DUMBBELL SHOULDER PRESS

1. Stand with feet straight ahead and shoulder-width apart.

2. Hold dumbbells at shoulder level, with palms facing out.

3. With arms slightly in front of ears, draw in belly button and press dumbbells overhead, fully extending arms.

4. Arms should be slightly in front of ears with belly button drawn in.

5. Hold, then slowly return dumbbells to start position.

6. Repeat as instructed.

Tips

- Maintain proper posture position throughout the entire exercise.

- Keep palms facing out throughout exercise.

SINGLE-LEG SQUAT

1. Stand with feet straight ahead and shoulder-width apart.

2. Get into proper posture position (abdominals drawn in, chest lifted, shoulders down, chin tucked) and place hands on hips.

3. Squeeze butt muscles, balance on one leg, and lift other leg directly beside it.

4. Slowly squat on one leg as if sitting into a chair, keep knee in line with toe.

5. Hold for 2 seconds, then slowly stand upright by pushing through heel.

6. Switch legs and repeat as instructed.

Tips

- Maintain proper posture position throughout the entire exercise.
- Keep shoulders and hips level.

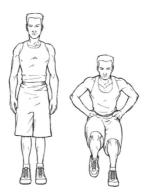

SPEED-AGILITY-QUICKNESS (SAQ) TRAINING

SAQ drills improve your overall game by conditioning your basketball footwork skills. These exercises also train your heart and lungs specifically for basketball so you will have the stamina you need to play your best for the entire game. Transitioning from offense to defense is one way SAQ is useful on the court. Grabbing rebounds and going coast-to-coast for lay-ups, making cuts to elude defenders, and dekeing out the man covering you with crossover dribbles also require skillful speed, agility and quickness. Remember,

- Speed is how fast you can move in one direction.
- Agility is your ability to start, stop, and change directions quickly, while maintaining good posture.
- Quickness is your ability to react to a stimulus and change the motion of your body.

After performing your workout preparation exercises on Tuesdays and Thursdays, you will do the following SAQ drills throughout each week of Stability Training.

SAQ ONE INS

1. Run straight through ladder, placing one foot in each box.
2. Pump arms, keep chest up, and land on balls of feet.

SAQ TWO INS

1. Run straight through ladder, placing two feet in each box.

2. Pump arms, keep chest up, and land on balls of feet.

SAQ OUT/OUT/IN/IN

1. Start with both feet in first box.

2. Step forward, moving right foot out of box; straddle ladder, placing left foot out of box.

3. Move right foot into next box in ladder; move left foot into same box.

4. Repeat moving forward with feet straddling out-out and in-in ladder.

SAQ T-DRILL

1. Place four cones in shape of "T," 5 yards between each.

2. Stand in a ready-to-run position at base of "T."

3. Sprint straight ahead to middle cone.

4. Side shuffle to outside cone.

5. Change direction and crossover step* (page 83) to far cone.

6. Change direction and side shuffle back to middle cone.

7. Backpedal to start position.

SAQ 10 IN 1 DRILL

10 in 1

Sprint from 1-2 and then back from 2-1, five times for a total of 10 lengths of court.
　　Objective is to get 10 lengths of court in 1 minute (10 in 1).
Rest 60 seconds after each 1-minute drill.

STABILITY TRAINING RUNDOWN

The next few pages combine all of the information provided in this chapter to give you a 4-week Stability Training program. As your body becomes conditioned from one week to the next, your workout variables will change to advance your workouts.

Once you have completed all 4 weeks of Stability Training, you will repeat the Self-Assessment in Chapter 6 to measure the progress you made in your total body strength, flexibility, power, speed, agility, and quickness. You will also reassess your muscle imbalances and customize the Foam Roll and Static Stretching exercises for your Strength Training workouts.

STABILITY TRAINING: WEEKS 1 AND 2

Training Component	Reps	Sets
Workout Preparation		
1. *Foam Roll Exercises* (per Chapter 6)	1	1
2. *Static Stretching Exercises* (per Chapter 6)	1	2
3. *Dynamic Warm-up Exercises* (Circuit Training)* Tube Walking: Side to Side Lunge Circuit Single-Leg Squat Touchdown Single-Leg Multiplanar Hop	12–15	1
4. *Core Exercises* (Circuit Training #4, 5, 6)* Side Iso-Abs	12–15	2
Floor Bridge with Alternate Leg	12–15	2
All Fours: Arm Opposite Leg	12–15	2
5. *Balance Exercise* Single-Leg Balance Reach	12–15	2
6. *Plyometric Exercise* Box Jump-up and Hold	8	2
Resistance Stability Training (Circuit Training)*		
1. Staggered-Stance Cable Chest Press	12–15	2
2. Standing Cable Row	12–15	2
3. Standing Dumbbell Shoulder Press	12–15	2
4. Single-Leg Squat	12–15	2

*__Circuit Training__—Perform the exercises in the section, one right after the other, with minimal rest (about 30 seconds); rest longer

MONDAY, WEDNESDAY, FRIDAY WORKOUTS

Training Intensity	Rep Tempo	Rest Interval
n/a	30 seconds hold	n/a
n/a	20 seconds hold	n/a
n/a	n/a	n/a
n/a	5–10 seconds hold	About 30 seconds
n/a	5–10 seconds hold	About 30 seconds
n/a	5–10 seconds hold	About 30 seconds
n/a	5–10 seconds hold	About 30 seconds
n/a	3–5 seconds hold	About 60 seconds between circuits
60–65%	(4–2–1)	About 30 seconds
60–65%	(4–2–1)	About 30 seconds
60–65%	(4–2–1)	About 30 seconds
60–65%	(4–2–1)	About 60 seconds between circuits

(about 60 seconds) after the series of exercises has been completed, and before the next set begins.

STABILITY TRAINING: WEEKS 1 AND 2

Speed-Agility-Quickness (SAQ) Training

Training Component	Reps	Sets
Workout Preparation		
1. *Foam Roll Exercises* (per Chapter 6)	1	1–2
2. *Static Stretching Exercises* (per Chapter 6)	1	2
3. *Dynamic Warm-up Exercises* (Circuit Training)* Tube Walking: Side to Side Lunge Circuit Single-Leg Squat Touchdown Single-Leg Multiplanar Hop	12–15	1
SAQ Speed Ladder Drills		
1. One Ins	n/a	2
2. Two Ins	n/a	2
3. Out/Out/In/In	n/a	2
SAQ Court Drills		
1. T-Drill	n/a	4
2. 10-in-1 Drill	n/a	1–2

*__Circuit Training__—Perform the exercises in the section, one right after the other, with minimal rest; resting longer

TUESDAY, THURSDAY WORKOUTS

Training Intensity	Rep Tempo	Rest Interval
n/a	30 seconds hold	n/a
n/a	20 seconds hold	n/a
n/a	n/a	n/a
n/a	(x–x–x)	n/a
n/a	(x–x–x)	n/a
n/a	(x–x–x)	About 30 seconds
n/a	(x–x–x)	About 30 seconds
n/a	(x–x–x)	About 60 seconds

(about 30 seconds) after the series of exercises has been completed, and before the next set begins.

STABILITY TRAINING: WEEKS 3 AND 4

Training Component	Reps	Sets
Workout Preparation		
1. *Foam Roll Exercises* (per Chapter 6)	1	1
2. *Static Stretching Exercises* (per Chapter 6)	1	2
3. *Dynamic Warm-up Exercises* *(Circuit Training)** Tube Walking: Side to Side Lunge Circuit Single-Leg Squat Touchdown Single-Leg Multiplanar Hop	12–15	1
4. *Core Exercises* (Circuit Training #4, 5, 6)* Side-Iso Abs	12–15	3
Floor Bridge with Alternate Leg All Fours: Arm Opposite Leg	12–15 12–15	3 3
5. *Balance Exercise* Single-Leg Balance Reach	12–15	3
6. *Plyometric Exercise* Box Jump-up and Hold	10	3
Resistance Stability Training (Circuit Training)*		
1. Staggered-Stance Cable Chest Press	12–15	3
2. Standing Cable Row	12–15	3
3. Standing Dumbbell Shoulder Press	12–15	3
4. Single-Leg Squat	12–15	3

__Circuit Training__—Perform the exercises in the section, one right after the other, with minimal rest (about 30 seconds);

MONDAY, WEDNESDAY, FRIDAY WORKOUTS

Training Intensity	Rep Tempo	Rest Interval
n/a	30 seconds hold	n/a
n/a	20 seconds hold	n/a
n/a	n/a	n/a
n/a	5–10 seconds hold	About 30 seconds
n/a	5–10 seconds hold	About 30 seconds
n/a	5–10 seconds hold	About 30 seconds
n/a	5–10 seconds hold	About 30 seconds
n/a	3–5 seconds hold	About 60 seconds between circuits
65%	(4-2-1)	About 30 seconds
65%	(4-2-1)	About 30 seconds
65%	(4-2-1)	About 30 seconds
65%	(4-2-1)	About 60 seconds between circuits

rest longer (about 60 seconds) after the series of exercises has been completed, and before the next set begins.

STABILITY TRAINING: WEEKS 3 AND 4

Speed-Agility-Quickness (SAQ) Training

Training Component	Reps	Sets
Workout Preparation		
1. *Foam Roll Exercises* (per Chapter 6)	1	1–2
2. *Static Stretching Exercises* (per Chapter 6)	1	2
3. *Dynamic Warm-up Exercises* (Circuit Training)* Tube Walking: Side to Side Lunge Circuit Single-Leg Squat Touchdown Single-Leg Multiplanar Hop	12–15	1
SAQ Speed Ladder Drills		
1. One Ins	n/a	3
2. Two Ins	n/a	3
3. Out/Out/In/In	n/a	3
SAQ Court Drills		
1. T-Drill	n/a	6
2. 10-in-1 Drill	n/a	3–4

*__Circuit Training__—Perform the exercises in the section, one right after the other, with minimal rest; rest longer

TUESDAY, THURSDAY WORKOUTS

Training Intensity	Rep Tempo	Rest Interval
n/a	30 seconds hold	n/a
n/a	20 seconds hold	n/a
n/a	n/a	n/a
n/a	(x–x–x)	n/a
n/a	(x–x–x)	n/a
n/a	(x–x–x)	About 30 seconds
n/a	(x–x–x)	About 30 seconds
n/a	(x–x–x)	About 60 seconds

(about 30 seconds) after the series of exercises has been completed, and before the next set begins.

KEY POINT

Stability training conditions the deep muscles you cannot see, the muscles that support your pelvis and spine. These muscles are the foundation muscles from which all movement is performed.

On the court, you use stability muscles when guarding, passing, shooting, and dribbling. You even use them with your strength muscles when boxing out from the paint, and with your power muscles when blocking a shot.

EIGHT
Strength Training

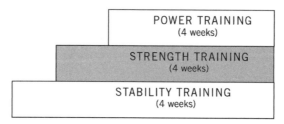

The OPT System

After four weeks of conditioning your stability muscles, you are now ready to train your *strength* muscles. Whereas the stability muscles are the muscles you cannot see— the deep muscles that support the spine and pelvis—the strength muscles are the larger muscles you can see when you look in the mirror, the major muscles like your chest, back, shoulders, and thighs.

The goal of Strength Training is to make your major muscles stronger and bigger so you can play more effectively on the court. You use these muscles in basketball with actions like posting someone up, setting picks, and boxing out from the paint.

This is a good time to remind you that strength movements require you to first contract your stability muscles. The reason is that your body's muscles work from the inside out. That means the deeper muscles must be contracted before the outer ones so that your spine will be supported before movement occurs.

Here are the workout components you will use in Strength Training (the details of these components are listed in the last few pages of this chapter).

STRENGTH TRAINING: WORKOUT COMPONENTS

See Chapter 4 for detailed definitions.

1. WORKOUT PREPARATION: Performed before every workout (Monday through Friday).

2. RESISTANCE STRENGTH TRAINING: Performed on Mondays, Wednesdays, and Fridays.

3. SPEED-AGILITY-QUICKNESS TRAINING: Performed on Tuesdays and Thursdays.

WORKOUT PREPARATION

Foam Roll and Static Stretching Exercises

Before beginning Strength Training, be sure to repeat the Overhead and Single-Leg Squat assessments in Chapter 6 to identify your muscle imbalances and determine the Foam Roll and Static Stretching exercises that you will perform to correct them during these next four weeks. Remember, these exercises will change as you go along through each phase of your OPT program, depending on the outcome of your Self-Assessment. You will do these exercises at the beginning of every single workout throughout each week of Strength Training. Illustrations for your Foam Roll and Static Stretching exercises are also listed in Chapter 6. These exercises are listed below.

Dynamic Warm-up Exercises

After the Foam Roll and Static Stretching exercises are completed, you will do the Dynamic Warm-up to actively stretch your muscles through their full range of motion. You will perform the same Dynamic Warm-up exercises in Strength Training that you did in Stability Training. Remember to do these exercises Monday through Friday at the beginning of every single workout throughout the entire phase.

TUBE WALKING: SIDE TO SIDE

1. Stand with feet hip-width apart, knees slightly bent, and feet straight ahead.

2. Place tubing around ankles.

3. Keep feet and knees pointing straight ahead and take small steps sideways.

4. Repeat in opposite direction.

Tips

- Maintain proper posture position throughout the entire exercise.
- Do not allow knees to cave in or feet to turn out.

LUNGE CIRCUIT

1. Stand with feet straight ahead and shoulder-width apart.

2. Hold dumbbell in each hand, palms facing side of body.

3. Lunge forward, landing on heel of lunge foot, foot straight ahead, knee bent at 90-degree angle. Back leg is also bent at 90-degree angle, heel lifted off floor.

4. Push off heel of front foot onto back leg.

5. Return to start position.

6. Lunge sideways; stabilize with lunge foot straight ahead, knee bent and directly over second and third toes; opposite leg straight with foot flat on ground.

7. Push off bent leg to return to start position.

8. Turn and lunge by opening hips and stepping back in 45-degree angle, pivoting on back foot.

9. Stabilize with front foot straight ahead, knee bent at 90-degree angle and directly over second and third toes; opposite leg bent at 90-degree angle, heel of back foot off ground.

10. Push off front foot to return to start position.

Tips

• Maintain proper posture position throughout the entire exercise.

• Avoid using momentum in this exercise. Perform the lunges with control.

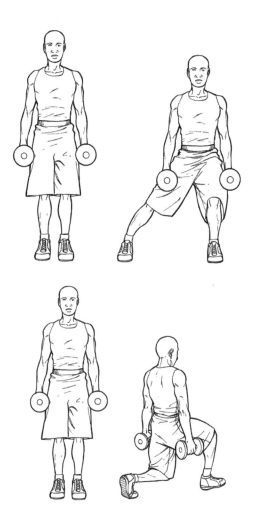

SINGLE-LEG SQUAT TOUCHDOWN

1. Stand with feet straight ahead and hip-width apart.

2. Stand in proper posture position (abdominals drawn in, chest lifted, shoulders down, chin tucked) and place hands on hips.

3. Squeeze butt muscles, balance on one leg, and lift other directly beside it.

4. Keep shoulders and hips level.

5. Slowly squat, bending hip and knee.

6. Reach opposite hand toward balance foot and hold for 2 seconds.

7. Pushing through heel, slowly return to start position.

8. Repeat as instructed.

9. Switch legs and repeat.

Tip

Maintain proper posture position throughout the entire exercise.

SINGLE-LEG MULTIPLANAR HOPS

1. Stand with feet straight ahead and shoulder-width apart.

2. Squeeze butt muscles, balance on right leg and lift left leg directly beside it, knee in line with toe.

3. Hop forward, landing on left foot. Stabilize and hold for 2 to 4 seconds.

4. Hop backward to start position, landing on right foot. Stabilize and hold for 2 to 4 seconds.

5. Switch legs and repeat.

6. Hop sideways, landing on left foot. Stabilize and hold for 2 to 4 seconds.

7. Hop sideways to start position, landing on right foot. Stabilize and hold for 2 to 4 seconds.

8. Hop turning back at 45-degree angle, landing on left foot. Stabilize and hold for 2 to 4 seconds.

9. Hop turning forward at 45-degree angle, landing on right foot to return to start position. Stabilize and hold for 2 to 4 seconds.

10. Switch legs and repeat.

11. Repeat steps 1 through 10 as instructed.

Tips

- Maintain proper posture position throughout the entire exercise.

- Avoid using momentum in this exercise. Perform the hops with control.

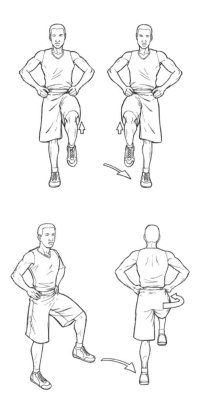

Core Exercises

The focus in Stability Training was conditioning your core's stability muscles, the muscles that keep the pelvis and spine in place. The exercises you used like the Side Iso-Abs required no movement of the spine. In Strength Training, the focus will be on conditioning your core's *strength* muscles, the muscles that move the spine. These exercises, however, require you to stabilize the spine before you move it so that injury will not occur. So the core exercises in Strength Training will require you to use both your stability and strength muscles.

You will do this by using a stability ball. What will happen if you do not contract your stability muscles before doing strength movements like flexion, extension, and rotation on the ball? Quite simply, you will fall off the ball! So you will us your strength muscles to do movements like ab crunches and back extensions, while using your stability muscles to keep yourself balanced on the ball.

Here are the core exercises you will do Monday through Friday throughout each week in Strength Training.

STABILITY BALL CRUNCH

1. Lie with ball under lower back and knees directly over ankles; feet on floor, hip-width apart.

2. Extend back over curve of ball and cross hands on chest.

3. Draw in belly button and squeeze butt muscles.

4. Slowly crunch upper body forward (ribs toward hips), raising shoulder blades off ball while keeping chin tucked toward chest.

5. Slowly lower upper body over ball, while keeping belly button drawn in.

6. Repeat as instructed.

STABILITY BALL BRIDGE

1. Lie with ball between shoulder blades and head resting on ball, hands on hips. Place feet on floor, hip-width apart.

2. Draw in belly button and squeeze butt muscles.

3. Lift pelvis until knees are in line with hips and shoulders (tabletop position).

4. Slowly lower pelvis toward floor and repeat as instructed.

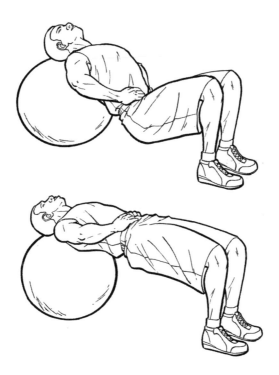

STABILITY BALL BACK EXTENSION

1. Lie with ball under midsection, feet pointed toward floor and legs straight.

2. Extend arms in front of ball.

3. Draw in belly button and squeeze butt muscles.

4. Pinch shoulder blades back and down to bring arms around to side of body.

5. Return arms to front of body.

6. Repeat as instructed.

Tip

Keep back and neck in proper alignment (ankles, knees, hips, shoulders, and ears all in alignment).

Balance Exercise

You use balance on the court with movements like a free throw, hook shot, and even the tip off. Balance enables you to extend straight up and place your entire body in the right position as you go through the shooting motion. Without good balance, you will either jump forward or backward, reducing the accuracy of your shot.

In Stability Training, you did the Single-Leg Balance Reach, which focused on the ability to balance with little or no movement (stability). Now it's time to begin training your ability to balance in motion. You will do this by using portions of basketball movements to strengthen basketball-specific muscles. For example, the balance exercise you will do in Strength Training is called Step-up to Balance, which conditions the same muscles as those used in a lay-up. This exercise requires you to contract your stability muscles first so you can strengthen your ability to balance through a greater range of motion.

Here is the balance exercise you will do Monday through Friday throughout each week in Strength Training.

STEP-UP TO BALANCE

1. Stand in front of a box or platform (6 to 18 inches high) with feet straight ahead and hip-width apart.

2. Get into proper posture position (abdominals drawn in, chest lifted, shoulders down, chin tucked).

3. Squeeze butt muscles and step onto box with one leg, bring opposite knee up by toes pointed straight ahead.

4. Stand upright and balance on same leg, bring opposite knee up by flexing hip and knee of leg.

5. Hold, then step both legs down to ground.

6. Repeat as instructed.

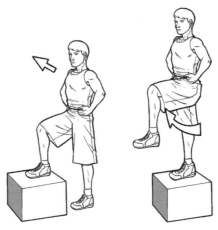

Plyometric Exercise

Plyometric exercises condition the muscles used for explosive basketball movements like jumping and landing. These exercises will be performed quickly and repeatedly to condition you for plays on the court that require similar movements. The Squat Jump, for example, requires you to squat then jump as high as you can in the air. As soon as you touch the ground you repeat the movement several times more to condition your explosive capabilities. You will perform the Squat Jump, illustrated below, after the balance exercise at the beginning of every workout throughout each week in Strength Training.

SQUAT JUMP

1. Stand with feet straight ahead and shoulder-width apart.
2. Get into proper posture position (abdominals drawn in, chest lifted, shoulders down, chin tucked).
3. Hold a basketball ball at chest level.
4. Squeeze butt muscles, squat and jump up, raising arms above head with basketball in hands.
5. Land softly with control on middle portion of foot, feet straight ahead, knees in line with toes.
6. Return basketball to chest level.
7. Repeat as instructed, spending as little time as possible on ground.

RESISTANCE STRENGTH TRAINING

Now that you have done the workout preparation exercises, your body is ready for the Resistance Training component of your workout. In this phase, you will use resistance to increase your *strength*. Why is it important to train for strength in the game of hoops? Because there are times when you need to hold your ground as a defender tries to push you out of the paint when you are trying to post up or when you are trying to set a pick to help a teammate make a shot. This requires strength, and the best way to condition for it is with resistance exercises. The goal in Strength Training is to train your major muscles like the chest, back, shoulder, and thighs to become larger and stronger.

You will use heavier weight, fewer reps, and more sets than you did for Stability Training. You will also use a superset technique. This means you will do two different exercises for the same muscle group, performed back-to-back with minimal rest. In Strength Training, you will superset a Strength exercise with a Stability exercise. The purpose is to continue conditioning the stability muscles that support your pelvis and spine, while also increasing the size and strength of your major muscles. Remember, you cannot effectively execute a strength movement without using your stability muscles.

Here is an outline of your Strength Training workout variables. They are also detailed in your workouts at the end of this chapter.

RESISTANCE STRENGTH WORKOUT VARIABLES

Reps	Sets	Intensity	Rep Tempo	Rest Interval
			Strength Set (2-0-2)	About 30 seconds between supersets
8–12	2–4	70–80% Max Effort		
			Stability Set (3-2-1)	About 90 seconds between circuits

See Chapter 5 for detailed definitions of workout variables.

Sets in these workouts are designed to be performed in a circuit training format, which means you will perform the exercises one right after the other, with approximately 30 seconds of rest in between. If you feel you have recovered before 30 seconds, you can continue with your next exercise. After the last exercise, you will rest for approximately 90 seconds then repeat the series of exercises over again as directed by the number of sets listed.

You will do the following chest, back, shoulder, and leg resistance exercises on Mondays, Wednesdays, and Fridays throughout each week in Strength Training.

CHEST SUPERSET: Perform Dumbbell Incline Chest Press immediately followed by Rotation Push-up.

DUMBBELL INCLINE CHEST PRESS

1. Lie with back on incline bench, feet straight ahead and flat on floor.

2. Hold dumbbell in each hand (palms facing away from body) at chest level, slightly outside of body with elbows flexed.

3. Draw in belly button.

4. Press both dumbbells up and together, fully extending arms and squeezing chest muscles.

5. Hold, then slowly return dumbbells to starting position.

6. Repeat as instructed.

ROTATION PUSH-UP

1. Begin with feet together and toes on floor; hands slightly wider than shoulder-width apart. Keep back flat—there should be a straight line from shoulders to hips to ankles.

2. Draw in belly button and squeeze butt muscles.

3. With flat back, slowly lower body toward floor, lowering and squeezing shoulder blades.

4. Push up to starting position.

5. Rotate body 90 degrees from floor, fully extending both arms—one in air and one stabilizing on floor.

6. Reverse movement of rotation to return to start position; repeat, alternating direction of rotation.

Note: This exercise can be modified by omitting the rotation (steps 5 and 6) and performing a traditional push-up, as described in steps 1 through 4. The traditional push-up can be performed on your knees for further modification.

BACK SUPERSET: Perform Standing Cable Extension immediately followed by Single-Leg Cable Row.

STANDING CABLE EXTENSION

1. Stand with feet straight ahead and knees slightly bent.

2. Get into proper posture position (abdominals drawn in, chest lifted, shoulders down, and chin tucked).

3. Grab a cable in each hand, arms extended in front of body at eye level.

4. Keep arms straight and bring extended arms to sides of body, palms facing down, and squeeze shoulder blades together.

5. Hold; return extended arms to start position.

6. Repeat as instructed.

SINGLE-LEG CABLE ROW

1. Stand on one leg facing cable machine, foot straight ahead.

2. Hold cable in each hand (palms facing inward), with arms extended at chest level.

3. Knees slightly bent, row by bringing thumbs toward armpits, squeeze shoulder blades together.

4. Hold; return to start position.

Tip

Do not shrug shoulders or jut head forward.

SHOULDER SUPERSET: Perform Standing Dumbbell Shoulder Press immediately followed by Single-Leg Dumbbell Scaption.

Standing Dumbbell Shoulder Press

1. Stand with feet straight ahead and shoulder-width apart.

2. Hold dumbbells at shoulder level, with palms facing out.

3. With arms slightly in front of ears, draw in belly button and press dumbbells over head, fully extending arms.

4. Arms should be slightly in front of ears with belly button drawn in.

5. Hold, then slowly return dumbbells to start position.

6. Repeat as instructed.

Tips

• Maintain proper posture position throughout the entire exercise.

• Keep palms facing out throughout exercise.

SINGLE-LEG DUMBBELL SCAPTION

1. Stand on one leg, foot straight ahead.

2. Get into proper posture position (abdominals drawn in, chest lifted, shoulders lowered, and chin tucked).

3. Hold dumbbell in each hand (palms facing side of body) with arms at side of body.

4. Raise both arms at 45-degree angle in front of body until hands reach eye level, thumbs up. Hold; return arms to side of body.

Tip

Do not shrug shoulders or arch back.

LEG SUPERSET: Perform Squat (preferred) or Leg Press immediately followed by Single-Leg Squat.

If you are not comfortable performing the Squat as illustrated, you can do the Leg Press instead.

SQUAT

1. Stand with feet straight ahead and shoulder-width apart; knees bent, hands on hips or behind ears.
2. Draw in belly button then squat as if sitting into a chair, bending knees and hips, and keeping feet straight. Allow butt muscles to "stick out" behind body.
3. Keep chest up, squeeze butt muscles, and press through heels to return to start; fully extend legs.
4. Repeat as instructed.

Tip

Do not arch back when squatting or allow knees to move in.

LEG PRESS

1. Stand in leg press machine; place back and butt muscles against support pads.

2. Place feet straight ahead and shoulder-width apart, knees slightly bent.

3. Squeeze butt muscles and lower into squat position.

4. Press through heels, pushing body upward by extending legs.

5. Push until legs are fully extended; repeat.

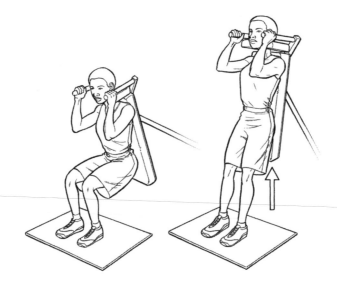

SINGLE-LEG SQUAT

1. Stand with feet straight ahead and shoulder-width apart.

2. Get into proper posture position (abdominals drawn in, chest lifted, shoulders down, chin tucked) and place hands on hips.

3. Squeeze butt muscles, balance on one leg, and lift other leg directly beside it.

4. Slowly squat on one leg as if sitting into a chair, keep knee in line with toe.

5. Hold for 2 seconds, then slowly stand upright by pushing through heel.

6. Switch legs and repeat as instructed.

Tips

- Maintain proper posture position throughout the entire exercise.

- Keep shoulders and hips level.

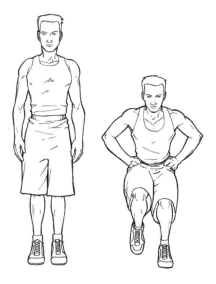

SPEED-AGILITY-QUICKNESS (SAQ) TRAINING

SAQ exercises will be done after the workout preparation exercises on Tuesdays and Thursdays. SAQ improves your running mechanics, speed, agility, and quickness. It also conditions your heart and lungs specifically for basketball.

The goal for SAQ in Strength Training is to begin training movement patterns that you use continuously on the court, such as "sprint-stop-change directions" and "backpedal-stop-side shuffle."

Here are the SAQ exercises you will perform on Tuesdays and Thursdays throughout each week of Strength Training.

SAQ ONE INS

1. Run straight through ladder, placing one foot in each box.
2. Pump arms, keep chest up, and land on balls of feet.

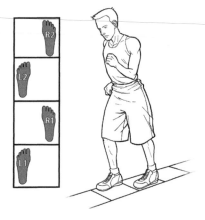

SAQ TWO INS

1. Run straight through ladder, placing two feet in each box.

2. Pump arms, keep chest up, and land on balls of feet.

SAQ OUT/OUT/IN/IN

1. Start with both feet in first box.

2. Step forward, moving right foot out of box; straddle ladder, placing left foot out of box.

3. Move right foot into next box in ladder; move left foot into same box.

4. Repeat moving forward with feet straddling out-out and in-in ladder.

SAQ IN/IN/OUT/OUT

1. Stand with body facing side of ladder.

2. Step forward into ladder placing left foot in box.

3. Bring right foot beside it into same box.

4. Step backward at diagonal with left foot out of ladder.

5. Bring right foot beside it out of ladder.

6. Repeat in-in-out-out movement, moving sideways through ladder.

7. Repeat in opposite direction.

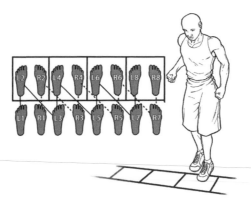

SAQ M-DRILL

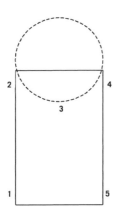

M-Drill

Sprint from baseline to elbow (1-2).
    Backpedal from elbow to middle of dotted circle (2-3).
    Sprint from middle of dotted circle to elbow (3-4).
    Backpedal from elbow to baseline (4-5).

SAQ LINE DRILL

Line Drill

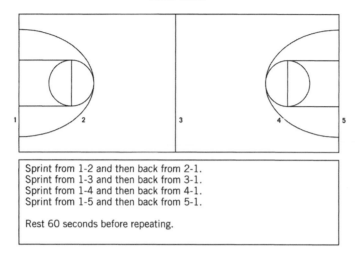

Sprint from 1-2 and then back from 2-1.
Sprint from 1-3 and then back from 3-1.
Sprint from 1-4 and then back from 4-1.
Sprint from 1-5 and then back from 5-1.

Rest 60 seconds before repeating.

STRENGTH TRAINING RUNDOWN

The next few pages combine all of the information provided in this chapter to give you a 4-week Strength Training program. As your body becomes conditioned from one week to the next, your workout variables will change to advance your workouts.

Once you have completed all 4 weeks of Strength Training, you will repeat the Self-Assessment in Chapter 6 to measure the progress you made with your total body strength, flexibility, power, speed, agility, and quickness. You will also reassess your muscle imbalances and customize the Foam Roll and Static Stretching exercises for your Power Training workouts.

STRENGTH TRAINING: WEEKS 1 AND 2

Training Component	Reps	Sets
Workout Preparation		
1. *Foam Roll Exercises* (per Chapter 6)	1	1
2. *Static Stretching Exercises* (per Chapter 6)	1	2
3. *Dynamic Warm-up Exercises* (Circuit Training)* Tube Walking: Side to Side Lunge Circuit Single-Leg Squat Touchdown Single-Leg Multiplanar Hop	12–15	1
4. *Core Exercises* (Circuit Train #4, 5, 6)* Stability Ball Crunch	12	2
Stability Ball Bridge Stability Ball Back Extension	12 12	2 2
5. *Balance Exercise* Step-up to Balance	12	2
6. *Plyometric Exercise* Squat Jump	8–10	2
Resistance Strength Training (Circuit Training)*		
1. Dumbbell Incline Chest Press/ 2. Rotation Push-up	10–12 each	2
3. Standing Cable Extension/ 4. Single-Leg Cable Row	10–12 each	2
5. Standing Dumbbell Shoulder Press/ Single-Leg Dumbbell Scaption	10–12 each	2
6. Squat (preferred) or Leg Press/ 7. Single-Leg Squat	10–12 each	2

*****Circuit Training**—*Perform the exercises in the section, one right after the other, with minimal rest (about 30 seconds between*

MONDAY, WEDNESDAY, FRIDAY WORKOUTS

Training Intensity	Rep Tempo	Rest Interval
n/a	30 seconds hold	n/a
n/a	20 seconds hold	n/a
n/a	n/a	n/a
n/a	(3-2-1)	About 30 seconds
n/a	(3-2-1)	About 30 seconds
n/a	(3-2-1)	About 30 seconds
n/a	5–10 seconds hold	About 30 seconds
n/a	3–5 seconds hold	About 90 seconds between circuits
70–75%	(2-0-2)/ (3-2-1)	About 30 seconds between supersets
70–75%	(2-0-2)/ (3-2-1)	About 30 seconds between supersets
70–75%	(2-0-2)/ (3-2-1)	About 30 seconds between supersets
70–75%	(2-0-2)/ (3-2-1)	About 90 seconds between supersets

supersets); rest longer (about 90 seconds) after the series of exercises has been completed, and before the next set begins.

STRENGTH TRAINING: WEEKS 1 AND 2

Speed-Agility-Quickness (SAQ) Training

Training Component	Reps	Sets
Workout Preparation		
1. *Foam Roll Exercises* (per Chapter 6)	1	1–2
2. *Static Stretching Exercises* (per Chapter 6)	1	2
3. *Dynamic Warm-up Exercises* (Circuit Training)* Tube Walking: Side to Side Lunge Circuit Single-Leg Squat Touchdown Single-Leg Multiplanar Hop	12–15	1
SAQ Speed Ladder Drills		
1. One Ins	n/a	2
2. Two Ins	n/a	2
3. Out/Out/In/In	n/a	2
4. In/In/Out/Out	n/a	2
SAQ Court Drills		
1. M-Drill	n/a	4–6
2. Line Drill	n/a	2–3

*__Circuit Training__—Perform the exercises in the section, one right after the other, with minimal rest; rest longer

TUESDAY AND THURSDAY WORKOUTS

Training Intensity	Rep Tempo	Rest Interval
n/a	30 seconds hold	n/a
n/a	20 seconds hold	n/a
n/a	n/a	n/a
n/a	(x–x–x)	n/a
n/a	(x–x–x)	n/a
n/a	(x–x–x)	n/a
n/a	(x–x–x)	About 30 seconds
n/a	(x–x–x)	About 60 seconds
n/a	(x–x–x)	About 30 seconds

(about 30 seconds) after the series of exercises has been completed, and before the next set begins.

STRENGTH TRAINING: WEEKS 3 AND 4

Training Component	Reps	Sets
Workout Preparation		
1. *Foam Roll Exercises* (per Chapter 6)	1	1
2. *Static Stretching Exercises* (per Chapter 6)	1	2
3. *Dynamic Warm-up Exercises* (Circuit Training)* Tube Walking: Side to Side Lunge Circuit Single-Leg Squat Touchdown Single-Leg Multiplanar Hop	12–15	1
4. *Core Exercises* (Circuit Train #4, 5, 6)*		
Stability Ball Crunch	10	3
Stability Ball Bridge	10	3
Stability Ball Back Extension	10	3
5. *Balance Exercise* Step-up to Balance	10	3
6. *Plyometric Conditioning Exercise* Squat Jump	10	3

MONDAY, WEDNESDAY, FRIDAY WORKOUTS

Training Intensity	Rep Tempo	Rest Interval
n/a	30 seconds hold	n/a
n/a	20 seconds hold	n/a
n/a	n/a	n/a
n/a	(3–2–1)	About 30 seconds
n/a	(3–2–1)	About 30 seconds
n/a	(3–2–1)	About 30 seconds
n/a	5–10 seconds hold	About 30 seconds
n/a	3–5 seconds hold	About 90 seconds between circuits

Continued

STRENGTH TRAINING: WEEKS 3 AND 4

Training Component	Reps	Sets
Resistance Strength Training (Circuit Training)*		
1. Dumbbell Incline Chest Press/ 2. Rotation Push-up	8 each	3–4
3. Standing Cable Extension/ 4. Single-Leg Cable Row	8 each	3–4
5. Standing Dumbbell Shoulder Press/ Single-Leg Dumbbell Scaption	8 each	3–4
6. Squat (preferred) or Leg Press/ 7. Single-Leg Squat	8 each	3–4

*__Circuit Training__—Perform the exercises in the section, one right after the other, with minimal rest (about 30 seconds between

MONDAY, WEDNESDAY, FRIDAY WORKOUTS

Training Intensity	Rep Tempo	Rest Interval
80%	(2–0–2)/ (3–2–1)	About 30 seconds between supersets
80%	(2–0–2)/ (3–2–1)	About 30 seconds between supersets
80%	(2–0–2)/ (3–2–1)	About 30 seconds between supersets
80%	(2–0–2)/ (3–2–1)	About 90 seconds between circuits

supersets); rest longer (about 90 seconds) after the series of exercises has been completed, and before the next set begins.

STRENGTH TRAINING: WEEKS 3 AND 4

Speed-Agility-Quickness (SAQ) Training

Training Component	Reps	Sets
Workout Preparation		
1. *Foam Roll Exercises* (per Chapter 6)	1	1–2
2. *Static Stretching Exercises* (per Chapter 6)	1–2	n/a
3. *Dynamic Warm-up Exercises* (Circuit Training)* Tube Walking: Side to Side Lunge Circuit Single-Leg Squat Touchdown Single-Leg Multiplanar Hop	12–15	1
SAQ Speed Ladder Drills		
1. One Ins	n/a	4
2. Two Ins	n/a	4
3. Out/Out/In/In	n/a	4
4. In/In/Out/Out	n/a	4
SAQ Court Drills		
1. M-Drill	n/a	8
2. Line Drill	n/a	4

*__Circuit Training__—Perform the exercises in the section, one right after the other, with minimal rest (about 30 seconds between

TUESDAY AND THURSDAY WORKOUTS

Training Intensity	Rep Tempo	Rest Interval
n/a	30 seconds hold	n/a
n/a	20 seconds hold	n/a
n/a	n/a	n/a
n/a	(x–x–x)	n/a
n/a	(x–x–x)	n/a
n/a	(x–x–x)	n/a
n/a	(x–x–x)	About 30 seconds
n/a	(x–x–x)	About 60 seconds
n/a	(x–x–x)	About 30 seconds

supersets); rest longer (about 90 seconds) after the series of exercises has been completed, and before the next set begins.

KEY POINT

Strength Training conditions the larger muscles you see when you look in the mirror—the major muscles like your chest, lats, shoulders, and thighs.

On the court, you use these muscles with actions like posting someone up, setting picks, and boxing out from the paint.

NINE
Power Training

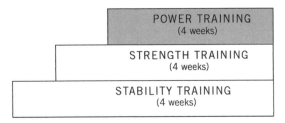

The OPT System

By the time you begin Power Training, you will have been training in the OPT system for 8 weeks (4 weeks of training in both Stability and Strength Training). Power Training is the *optimum* in the Optimum Performance Training system, because it uses both stability and strength muscles to perform power moves.

Power muscles need to be recruited quickly for explosive moves like a dunk, a quick step to take someone off the dribble, or a cut into the passing lanes to make a steal. Conditioning them requires lifting heavy weight in a controlled manner immediately followed by a fast movement with light weight that simulates an actual basketball move. The superset technique used in Strength Training will be introduced again in the Power Training resistance exercises. In this phase, you will superset a Strength exercise with a Power exercise.

The workout components you will use in Power Training are listed below. The details of these components are outlined in the last few pages of this chapter.

POWER TRAINING: WORKOUT COMPONENTS

See Chapter 4 for detailed definitions.

1. WORKOUT PREPARATION: Performed before every workout (Monday through Friday).

2. RESISTANCE POWER TRAINING: Performed on Monday, Wednesday, and Friday.

3. SPEED-AGILITY-QUICKNESS TRAINING: Performed on Tuesday and Thursday.

WORKOUT PREPARATION

Foam Roll and Static Stretching Exercises

As you now know, the knots in your muscles must be released so that you can stretch your muscles back to their normal length before beginning your active workout. That's why you will continue doing Foam Roll and Static Stretching exercises, Monday through Friday before every single workout in Power Training. Before beginning this phase, remember to reassess your muscle imbalances with the Overhead and Single-Leg Squat Assessments (Chapter 6) and determine which Foam Roll and Static Stretching exercises you will perform throughout Power Training to correct them. Illustrations for these exercises are also listed in Chapter 6.

Dynamic Warm-up Exercises

You will continue doing the same Dynamic Warm-up exercises in Power Training that you did in Stability and Strength Training to prepare and train your body to work in the range, speed, and direction of motion that will be used in the rest of your workout. These exercises will continue to be done Monday through Friday, before every single workout; they are listed below.

TUBE WALKING: SIDE TO SIDE

1. Stand with feet hip-width apart, knees slightly bent, and feet straight ahead.

2. Place tubing around ankles.

3. Keep feet and knees pointing straight ahead and take small steps sideways.

4. Repeat in opposite direction.

Tips

- Maintain proper posture position throughout the entire exercise.

- Do not allow knees to cave in or feet to turn out.

LUNGE CIRCUIT

1. Stand with feet straight ahead and shoulder-width apart.

2. Hold dumbbell in each hand, palms facing side of body.

3. Lunge forward, landing on heel of lunge foot, foot straight ahead, knee bent at 90-degree angle. Back leg is also bent at 90-degree angle, heel lifted off floor.

4. Push off heel of front foot onto back leg.

5. Return to start position.

6. Lunge sideways; stabilize with lunge foot straight ahead, knee bent and directly over second and third toes; opposite leg straight with foot flat on ground.

7. Push off bent leg to return to start position.

8. Turn and lunge by opening hips and stepping back in 45-degree angle, pivoting on back foot.

9. Stabilize with front foot straight, knee bent at 90-degree angle and directly over second and third toes; opposite leg bent at 90-degree angle, heel of back foot off ground.

10. Push off front foot to return to start position.

Tips

- Maintain proper posture position throughout the entire exercise.

- Avoid using momentum in this exercise. Perform the lunges with control.

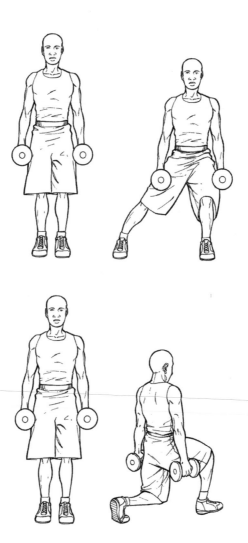

SINGLE-LEG SQUAT TOUCHDOWN

1. Stand with feet straight ahead and hip-width apart.

2. Stand in proper posture position (abdominals drawn in, chest lifted, shoulders down, chin tucked) and place hands on hips.

3. Squeeze butt muscles, balance on one leg, and lift other directly beside it.

4. Keep shoulders and hips level.

5. Slowly squat, bending hip and knee.

6. Reach opposite hand toward balance foot and hold for 2 seconds.

7. Pushing through heel, slowly return to start position.

8. Repeat as instructed.

9. Switch legs and repeat.

Tip

Maintain proper posture position throughout the entire exercise.

SINGLE-LEG MULTIPLANAR HOPS

1. Stand with feet straight ahead and shoulder-width apart.

2. Squeeze butt muscles, balance on right leg and lift left leg directly beside it, knee in line with toe.

3. Hop forward, landing on left foot. Stabilize and hold for 2 to 4 seconds.

4. Hop backward to start position, landing on right foot. Stabilize and hold for 2 to 4 seconds.

5. Switch legs and repeat.

6. Hop sideways, landing on left foot. Stabilize and hold for 2 to 4 seconds.

7. Hop sideways to start position, landing on right foot. Stabilize and hold for 2 to 4 seconds.

8. Hop turning back at 45-degree angle, landing on left foot. Stabilize and hold for 2 to 4 seconds.

9. Hop turning forward at 45-degree angle, landing on right foot to return to start position. Stabilize and hold for 2 to 4 seconds.

10. Switch legs and repeat.

11. Repeat step 1 through 10 above as instructed.

Tips

- Maintain proper posture position throughout the entire exercise.

- Avoid using momentum in this exercise. Perform the hops with control.

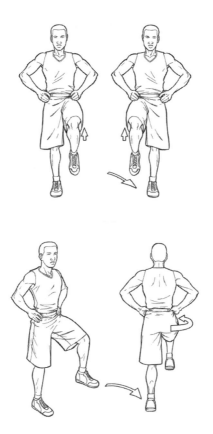

You will not perform specific Core, Balance, and Plyometric exercises in Power Training as you did in Stability and Strength Training because these movements are actually incorporated into the resistance exercises you will perform in this phase.

RESISTANCE POWER TRAINING

Power is your ability to produce the greatest amount of force in the shortest amount of time. You use power on the court when you bang the boards, take a pass and immediately go up for a jumper, and when you make a cut to avoid a defender. Resistance

Power Training exercises condition you to quickly catch the ball, load, and explode—decreasing your chances of having a defender block your shot.

Power Training resistance exercises require you to apply the stability and strength gains you have made in Stability and Strength Training to speeds and forces that are more realistic to basketball. You will use the superset technique again in Power Training. This time you will superset a Strength exercise with a Power exercise that simulates an actual explosive basketball move. You will also use lower reps, higher sets, and longer rest periods between circuits than you did for Stability and Strength Training.

Here is a rundown of your Power Training workout variables. They are also detailed in your workouts at the end of this chapter.

RESISTANCE POWER WORKOUT VARIABLES

Reps	Sets	Intensity	Rep Tempo	Rest Interval
Strength Set 1–5	3–5	**Strength Set** 85–100% Max	**Strength Set** (2–0–2)	About 30 seconds between supersets
Power Set 8–10		**Power Set** 2–5% Body Weight	**Power Set** Explosive (x–x–x)	About 2 minutes between circuits

See Chapter 5 for detailed definitions of workout variables.

Don't let the different training intensities in this phase confuse you. Remember that you will superset a Strength exercise with a Power exercise. Strength exercises require a maximum intensity of 85 to 100 percent. The Power exercises you will do involve throwing and passing a medicine ball with explosive energy. The intensity for medicine ball training is listed as a percentage of your body weight (2 to 5 percent).

Sets in these workouts are designed to be performed in a circuit training format, which means you will perform the exercises one right after the other, with approximately 30 seconds rest in between. If you feel you have recovered before 30 seconds, you can continue with your next exercise. After the last exercise, you will rest for approximately 2 minutes then repeat the series of exercises over again as directed by the number of sets listed.

Using the workout variables listed above, you will do the following exercises on Mondays, Wednesdays, and Fridays throughout each week of Power Training.

CHEST SUPERSET: Perform Staggered-Stance Cable Chest Press immediately followed by Medicine Ball Rotation Pass.

STAGGERED-STANCE CABLE CHEST PRESS

1. Stand with back to weight stack, feet straight ahead and in a staggered stance (back leg straight, front leg bent).

2. Hold a cable in each hand at chest level (palms facing down), elbows bent and slightly below shoulder level.

3. Press both cables forward and together, fully extending arms and squeezing chest muscles.

4. Slowly return hands to start position.

Tips

- Maintain proper posture position throughout the entire exercise.

- Do not allow head to jut forward or shoulders to rise toward ears.

MEDICINE BALL ROTATION PASS

The weight of your medicine ball should be 2 to 5 percent of your body weight.

1. Stand with body turned at 90-degree angle from wall, feet straight ahead and shoulder-width apart.

2. Hold medicine ball with both hands at chest level with elbows flexed.

3. Squeeze butt muscles and rotate body quickly and explosively toward wall, pivoting back leg as body turns.

4. With arm farthest from wall, use entire upper body to push and release ball toward wall as hard as possible; do not allow shoulders to shrug.

5. Catch ball; repeat as quickly as possible with control.

BACK SUPERSET: Perform Standing Cable Row immediately followed by Overhead Medicine Ball Throw.

STANDING CABLE ROW

1. Stand facing a cable machine with feet straight ahead and shoulder-width apart.

2. Hold cables with palms facing inward and arms extended at chest level.

3. With knees and hips slightly bent, row by bringing thumbs toward armpits, squeezing shoulder blades together.

4. Hold, then return to start position.

5. Repeat as instructed.

Tips

- Maintain proper posture position throughout the entire exercise.

- Do not allow head to jut forward or shoulders to rise toward ears.

OVERHEAD MEDICINE BALL THROW

The weight of your medicine ball shouold be 2 to 5 percent of your body weight.

1. Face wall with feet straight ahead and shoulder-width apart.

2. Get into proper posture position (belly button drawn in, chest lifted, shoulders down, and chin tucked).

3. Hold medicine ball overhead.

4. Squeeze butt muscles and throw medicine ball against wall, continue extending arms down past sides of body.

5. Catch ball; quickly repeat with control.

6. Repeat as instructed.

Tip

Do not allow back to arch.

SHOULDER EXERCISE: Perform Standing Dumbbell Shoulder Press.

To protect your rotator cuff muscles, you will not superset a Strength Exercise with a Power Exercise for your shoulders.

STANDING DUMBBELL SHOULDER PRESS

1. Stand with feet straight ahead and shoulder-width apart.

2. Hold dumbbells at shoulder level, with palms facing out.

3. With arms slightly in front of ears, draw in belly button and press dumbbells overhead, fully extending arms.

4. Arms should be slightly in front of ears with belly button drawn in.

5. Hold, then slowly return dumbbells to start position.

6. Repeat as instructed.

Tips

- Maintain proper posture position throughout the entire exercise.

- Keep palms facing out throughout exercise.

LEG SUPERSET: Perform Squat (preferred) or Leg Press immediately followed by Squat Jumps.

If you are not comfortable performing the Squat as illustrated, you can do the Leg Press instead.

SQUAT

1. Stand with feet straight ahead and shoulder-width apart; knees bent, hands on hips or behind ears.

2. Draw in belly button then squat as if sitting into a chair, bending knees and hips, and keeping feet straight ahead. Allow butt muscles to "stick out" behind body.

3. Keep chest up, squeeze butt muscles, and press through heels to return to start; fully extend legs.

4. Repeat as instructed.

Tip

Do not arch back when squatting or allow knees to move in.

LEG PRESS

1. Stand in leg press machine; place back and butt muscles against support pads.

2. Place feet straight ahead and shoulder-width apart, knees slightly bent.

3. Squeeze butt muscles and lower into squat position.

4. Press through heels, pushing body upward by extending legs.

5. Push until legs are fully extended; repeat.

SQUAT JUMP

1. Stand with feet straight ahead and shoulder-width apart.

2. Get into proper posture position (abdominals drawn in, chest lifted, shoulders down, chin tucked).

3. Hold a basketball ball at chest level.

4. Squeeze butt muscles, squat, and jump up, raising arms above head with basketball in hands.

5. Land softly with control on middle portion of foot with feet straight ahead, knees in line with toes.

6. Return basketball to chest level.

7. Repeat as instructed, spending as little time as possible on ground.

SPEED-AGILITY-QUICKNESS (SAQ) TRAINING

In Power Training, you will continue doing several of the SAQ exercises that you did in Stability and Strength Training, with a few more added in to kick up your SAQ skill a notch or two for specific basketball play. These drills will improve your ability to sprint the entire length of the floor (speed); perform a pick-and-roll where you set a screen then pivot toward the basket to receive a pass (agility); and do a give-and-go where you pass to a teammate and make a cut toward the basket to receive a return pass (quickness).

The SAQ exercises listed below will be performed after workout preparation exercises on Tuesdays and Thursdays throughout Power Training.

SAQ ONE INS

1. Run straight through ladder, placing one foot in each box.
2. Pump arms, keep chest up, and land on balls of feet.

SAQ TWO INS

1. Run straight through ladder, placing two feet in each box.

2. Pump arms, keep chest up, and land on balls of feet.

SAQ OUT/OUT/IN/IN

1. Start with both feet in first box.

2. Step forward, moving right foot out of box; straddle ladder, placing left foot out of box.

3. Move right foot into next box in ladder; move left foot into same box.

4. Repeat moving forward with feet straddling out-out and in-in ladder.

SAQ IN/IN/OUT/OUT

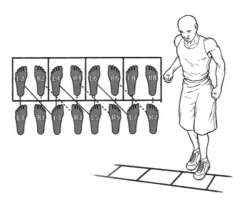

1. Stand with body facing side of ladder.

2. Step forward into ladder placing left foot in box.

3. Bring right foot beside it into same box.

4. Step backward at diagonal with left foot out of ladder.

5. Bring right foot beside it out of ladder.

6. Repeat in-in-out-out movement, moving sideways through ladder.

7. Repeat in opposite direction.

SAQ LEFT TEST

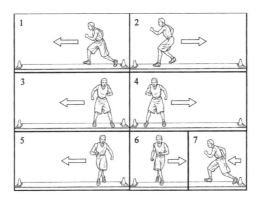

1. Place two cones 10 yards apart.

2. Stand in ready to run position at one cone.

3. Sprint to opposite cone, backpedal to start.

4. Side shuffle to opposite cone, side shuffle to start.

5. Crossover step* to opposite cone, crossover step to start.

6. Rest 45 seconds.

*See page 83 for definition.

POWER TRAINING RUNDOWN

The next few pages combine all of the information provided in this chapter to give you a detailed 4-week Power Training program. As your body becomes conditioned from one week to the next, your workout variables will change to advance your workouts.

Once you have completed all 4 weeks of Power Training, you will repeat the Self-Assessment in Chapter 6 to measure the progress you made with your total body strength, flexibility, power, speed, agility, and quickness. You will also reassess your muscle imbalances and customize the Foam Roll and Static Stretching exercises for your Stability Training workouts. Remember, after this phase, you will restart the 12-week OPT program from the beginning with Stability Training.

KEY POINT

Power Training is the peak of the OPT system because it uses stability and strength muscles to perform power moves.

On the court, you use power muscles for explosive moves like a dunk, a cut through the paint, or blocking a shot.

POWER TRAINING: WEEKS 1 AND 2

Training Component	Reps	Sets
Workout Preparation		
1. *Foam Roll Exercises* (per Chapter 6)	1	1
2. *Static Stretching Exercises* (per Chapter 6)	1	1
3. *Dynamic Warm-up Exercises* (Circuit Training)* Tube Walking: Side to Side Lunge Circuit Single-Leg Squat Touchdown Single-Leg Multiplanar Hop	12–15	1
Resistance Power Training (Circuit Training)*		
1. Staggered-Stance Cable Chest Press/ 2. Medicine Ball Rotation Pass	5 Strength 10 Power	3
3. Standing Cable Row/ 4. Overhead Medicine Ball Throw	5 Strength 10 Power	3
5. Standing Shoulder Press	5 Strength	3
6. Squat (preferred) or Leg Press/ 7. Squat Jump	5 Strength 10 Power	3

*__Circuit Training__—Perform the exercises in the section, one right after the other, with minimal rest (about 30 seconds between

**__BW__ = body weight

MONDAY, WEDNESDAY, FRIDAY WORKOUTS

Training Intensity	Rep Tempo	Rest Interval
n/a	30 seconds hold	n/a
n/a	20 seconds hold	n/a
n/a	30 seconds hold	n/a
Strength Set 85–89% Max Power Set 2–3% BW**	(2–0–2) (x–x–x)	About 30 seconds between supersets
Strength Set 85–89% Max Power Set 2–3% BW**	(2–0–2) (x–x–x)	About 30 seconds between supersets
Strength Set 85–89% Max	(2–0–2)	About 30 seconds between supersets
Strength Set 85–89% Max Power Set 2–3% BW**	(2–0–2) (x–x–x)	About 2 minutes between circuits

supersets); rest longer (about 2 minutes after the series of exercises has been completed, and before the next set begins).

POWER TRAINING: WEEKS 1 AND 2

Speed-Agility-Quickness (SAQ) Training

Training Component	Reps	Sets
Workout Preparation		
1. *Foam Roll Exercises* (per Chapter 6)	1	1–2
2. *Static Stretching Exercises* (per Chapter 6)	1	2
3. *Dynamic Warm-up Exercises* (Circuit Training)* Tube Walking: Side to Side Lunge Circuit Single-Leg Squat Touchdown Single-Leg Multiplanar Hop	12–15	1
SAQ Speed Ladder Drills		
1. One Ins	n/a	2
2. Two Ins	n/a	2
3. Out/Out/In/In	n/a	2
4. In/In/Out/Out	n/a	2
SAQ Court Drills		
1. LEFT	n/a	2–3

*__Circuit Training__—Perform the exercises in the section, one right after the other, with minimal rest; rest longer

TUESDAY AND THURSDAY WORKOUTS

Training Intensity	Rep Tempo	Rest Interval
n/a	30 seconds hold	n/a
n/a	20 seconds hold	n/a
n/a	n/a	n/a
n/a	(x–x–x)	n/a
n/a	(x–x–x)	n/a
n/a	(x–x–x)	n/a
n/a	(x–x–x)	About 30 seconds
n/a	(x–x–x)	About 45 seconds

(about 30 seconds) after the series of exercises has been completed, and before the next set begins.

POWER TRAINING: WEEKS 3 AND 4

Training Component	Reps	Sets
Workout Preparation		
1. *Foam Roll Exercises* (per Chapter 6)	1	1
2. *Static Stretching Exercises* (per Chapter 6)	1	1
3. *Dynamic Warm-up Exercises* (Circuit Training)* Tube Walking: Side to Side Lunge Circuit Single-Leg Squat Touchdown Single-Leg Multiplaner Hop	12–15	1
Resistance Power Training (Circuit Training)*		
1. Staggered-Stance Cable Chest Press/ 2. Medicine Ball Rotation Pass	4 Strength 8 Power	4
3. Standing Cable Row/ 4. Overhead Medicine Ball Throw	4 Strength 8 Power	4
5. Standing Dumbbell Shoulder Press	4 Strength	4
6. Squat (preferred) or Leg Press/ 7. Squat Jumps	4 Strength 8 Power	4

*****Circuit Training**—Perform the exercises in the section, one right after the other, with minimal rest (about 30 seconds between

******BW** = body weight

MONDAY, WEDNESDAY, FRIDAY WORKOUTS

Training Intensity	Rep Tempo	Rest Interval
n/a	30 seconds hold	n/a
n/a	20 seconds hold	n/a
n/a	30 seconds hold	n/a
Strength Set 89–93% Max Power Set 3–4% BW**	(2–0–2) (x–x–x)	About 30 seconds between supersets
Strength Set 89–93% Max Power Set 3–4% BW**	(2–0–2) (x–x–x)	About 30 seconds between supersets
Strength Set 89–93% Max	(2–0–2)	About 30 seconds between supersets
Strength Set 89–93% Max Power Set 3–4% BW**	(2–0–2) (x–x–x)	About 2 minutes between circuits

supersets); rest longer (about 2 minutes) after the series of exercises has been completed, and before the next set begins.

POWER TRAINING: WEEKS 3 AND 4

Speed-Agility-Quickness (SAQ) Training

Training Component	Reps	Sets
Workout Preparation		
1. *Foam Roll Exercises* (per Chapter 6)	1	1–2
2. *Static Stretching Exercises* (per Chapter 6)	1	2
3. *Dynamic Warm-up Exercises* (Circuit Training)* Tube Walking Side to Side Lunge Circuit Single-Leg Squat Touchdown Single-Leg Multiplanar Hop	12–15	1
SAQ Speed Ladder Drills		
1. One Ins	n/a	4
2. Two Ins	n/a	4
3. Out/Out/In/In	n/a	4
4. In/In/Out/Out	n/a	4
SAQ Court Drills		
1. LEFT	n/a	4–5

*__Circuit Training__—Perform the exercises in the section, one right after the other, with minimal rest; rest longer

TUESDAY AND THURSDAY WORKOUTS

Training Intensity	Rep Tempo	Rest Interval
n/a	30 seconds hold	n/a
n/a	20 seconds hold	n/a
n/a	n/a	n/a
n/a	(x–x–x)	n/a
n/a	(x–x–x)	n/a
n/a	(x–x–x)	n/a
n/a	(x–x–x)	About 30 seconds
n/a	(x–x–x)	About 45 seconds

(about 30 seconds) after the series of exercises has been completed, and before the next set begins.

TEN

Final Thoughts

At this point, you have finished your first 12-week cycle of OPT and have likely seen some impressive progress in strength, flexibility, power, speed, agility, and quickness since your first Self-Assessment. There's no doubt that you have fewer muscle imbalances, you're jumping higher, and you've knocked seconds off your SAQ drills. Congratulations!

Even though you may have reached a personal best after completing one 12-week cycle, you may not have reached your *best* yet. So the fun has just begun. To reach and maintain *optimum* performance, you have to continuously repeat the 12-week OPT System. After training with fast, explosive movements in Power Training, it may seem difficult to slow down the pace and lighten the weight with Stability Training. But this is exactly what your body needs to do. Your stability muscles must be restimulated to prepare your support system for the higher level of demand you'll place on it during the Strength and Power Training phases of the next 12-week cycle.

It's the continuous cycle of Stability, Strength, and Power Training that gives NBA teams and players using the OPT System the edge on the court. It is the reason the Phoenix Suns players lead the NBA in the fewest games missed due to injury and the reason their starters perform in 97 percent of regular season games. It is why great players like Steve Nash, Shaquille O'Neal, Kevin Garnett, Stephon Marbury, Amare Stoudemire, Emeka Okafor, and Shawn Marion are named as NBA All-Star players, Most Valuable Player, or Rookie of the Year.

Now it's your turn to be a great player. So flip back to Chapter 7 and begin Stability Training all over again, this time with heavier weight and higher intensity. Remember to focus on a slow rep tempo with Stability Training. You're just coming out of Power Training so you may be tempted to rush the reps. Slow motion is key in Stability Training.

Also remember that identifying and correcting muscle imbalances is the most important step in the OPT program. If your muscles and joints are not functioning *optimally*, you will never be able to condition yourself for *optimum* performance on the court. Stick with the Self-Assessments after completing each phase so you can adjust your Foam Roll and Static Stretching exercises to correct and prevent these muscle imbalances.

Remember that you can log on to www.OPT-online.info to download Self-Assessment forms and charts to use as you cycle through your OPT program again.

Good luck and thank you for experiencing OPT for Basketball. We hope it will change your game and your fitness level the way it has with the athletes who have followed this system as outlined in this book.

ACKNOWLEDGMENTS

SPECIAL THANKS TO THE FOLLOWING FOR MAKING THIS BOOK POSSIBLE:

Judith Regan

Doug Grad

Alison Stoltzfus

Scott Dalrymple

National Academy of Sports Medicine

National Basketball Athletic Trainers Association

Aaron Nelson

NOTES

NOTES

NOTES

NOTES

NOTES

NOTES